How to Write Your First Novel

Visit our How To website at www.howto.co.uk

At www.howto.co.uk you can engage in conversation with our authors – all of whom have 'been there and done that' in their specialist fields. You can get access to special offers and additional content but most importantly you will be able to engage with, and become a part of, a wide and growing community of people just like yourself.

At www.howto.co.uk you'll be able to talk and share tips with people who have similar interests and are facing similar challenges in their lives. People who, just like you, have the desire to change their lives for the better – be it through moving to a new country, starting a new business, growing their own vegetables, or writing a novel.

At www.howto.co.uk you'll find the support and encouragement you need to help make your aspirations a reality.

You can go direct to www.how-to-write-your-first-novel.co.uk which is part of the main How To site.

How To Books strives to present authentic, inspiring, practical information in their books. Now, when you buy a title from **How To Books,** you get even more than just words on a page.

Creative Writing

How to
Write Your
First Novel

Sophie King

howtobooks

Published by How To Books Ltd,
Spring Hill House, Spring Hill Road,
Begbroke, Oxford OX5 1RX. United Kingdom.
Tel: (01865) 375794. Fax: (01865) 379162.
info@howtobooks.co.uk
www.howtobooks.co.uk

How To Books greatly reduce the carbon footprint of their books by sourcing their
typesetting and printing in the UK.

British Library Cataloguing in Publication Data
A catalogue record for this book is available from the British Library

ISBN 978 1 84528 388 9

Produced for How To Books by Deer Park Productions, Tavistock, Devon
Typeset by PDQ Typesetting, Newcastle-under-Lyme, Staffs.
Printed and bound by Bell & Bain Ltd, Glasgow

NOTE: The material contained in this book is set out in good faith for general guidance
and no liability can be accepted for loss or expense incurred as a result of relying in
particular circumstances on statements made in the book. The laws and regulations are
complex and liable to change, and readers should check the current position with the
relevant authorities before making personal arrangements.

Mixed Sources
Product group from well-managed
forests and other controlled sources
www.fsc.org Cert no. TT-COC-002769
© 1996 Forest Stewardship Council

To my husband Shaun who has shown
me the 'How To' of life

Also to my children and my wonderful students
aged 8 to 89

Contents

Introduction   xi

1   Are You Ready to Commit?   **1**
Writing every day   2
Finding your best writing time   4
Yes – writing *is* working!   6
Writers' block   7
Writing tools   10
Are you sitting comfortably?   11
How do you know it's not a waste of time?   12
How to give yourself more writing time each day   13

2   A Novel Idea!   **16**
How to think of that winning idea   16
Tricks and tips on how to find a novel idea   17
Still not sure your idea will work?   34

3   Finding Your Voice   **37**
But how can your find yours?   38

4   The Killer First Sentence   **46**
So how do you come up with one of your own?   46
Can you live up to the promise of that first sentence?   49
Full circle   51

5   It's All in the Plot: Part One   **54**
What's your problem?   54
I don't believe it!   56
What is a sub-plot and do I need one?   57
The mechanics of plotting   58
Plotting a book – the Sophie King way!   59

6   It's All in the Plot: Part Two   **68**
The A–Z method   68
Throw and scatter method   71
Feeling board?   72

Tree diagram   72
Plotting your beginnings and endings   78
Does an ending need to be happy?   79
Research   80
How to plot flashbacks   80

7   Who Are You? How to Create Convincing Characters   83
What's their problem?   85
Who's who?   88
Are they believable?   89
My family and other animals   92
Make the most of your baddy   93
Minor characters   94
First date rule   94
Choosing a name   94
Have you missed their birthday?   95
How well do you know your character?   97
Going back to the beginning   98

8   Viewpoint   101
First person, third person or omniscient narrator?   107
Combining plot and viewpoint   114

9   De-mystifying Dialogue   118
Too much dialogue?   118
Too little dialogue?   119
How to make dialogue sound natural   121
Show and don't tell   125
Accents   126
Grammar   127

10 Setting   131
Going abroad   132
Don't overdo it!   133
Trawl your memory   135

11 How to Show and Not Tell   138
Use strong words and phrases   138
Internal dialogue   139
Doctor, doctor!   140
Double-checking!   141

Watch your language! 142
Get inside your character's head 142

12 Sense and Sensibility **147**
Smell 147
Colour 148
Sound 148
Touch 149
Taste 149

13 Humour **153**
Humorous example 155

14 Different Genres **158**
Historicals 159
Contemporary romantic fiction 159
Crime and thrillers 159
Sci-fi 159

15 How to Keep a Timeline **161**
Special occasions 162
Seasons of the year 163
Counting down the years 164

16 The Art of Revision **166**
Print out 167
Read out aloud 167
The red pen 167
Computer hassles 168
To cut or not to cut? 168
Enjoy it! 169

17 Synopsis **171**

18 The Title **175**
Tips on how to choose your title 175

19 Revealing All! **179**
Writers' courses and groups – good idea? 180
Literary consultancies 181
Literary festivals 181
Writers' holidays 182

20 How to Get Published   **183**
    If at first...   184
    Do you need an agent?   186
    Romantic Novelists Association   186
    The internet   186
    Competitions   187
    Dealing with rejection   187
    Self-publishing   189

21 Writing the Next Novel   **193**

22 Don't Skip This! It Might Help   **195**
    Definitions   195
    Commonly asked questions   196
    Useful organisations   198

Index   201

Introduction

‘ *I've always felt I had a book in me!* ’

How often have you said that but never actually got round to it? It's very understandable if you have. After all, it takes time to write a novel and time is something that very few of us have! Life has a habit of getting in the way. We get married perhaps and our partners expect us to be around in the evening instead of shutting ourselves away in a room to write. We have demanding jobs that mean we get home too late and too tired to write. We have children maybe, who take up all our time and attention.

So how on earth do we fit a novel in?

The good news is that it can be done – and that you can still hang on to all those other important things in your life too. But it does require a bit of shifting and that's what this book will help you do!

How to Write Your First Novel will give you advice on:

◆ how to re-organise your day and evening to give you writing time

◆ how to find your best writing time

◆ how to get a brilliant idea for your first novel

◆ how to create characters that will make your novel come alive

- how to plot your novel so that the reader simply HAS to turn the page

- how to understand viewpoint (don't worry about that one, right now!)

- how to make your characters talk realistically instead of 'school play' dialogue

- how to find your 'voice'

- how to Show and Not Tell

- how to create a realistic setting so we feel we are there.

And – most importantly! – tips and tricks on how to get published.

How to Write Your First Novel is a summary of all the lessons I learned, before my first novel was published. (I've had four more published since then.) It also has advice from other published writers, authors and agents.

It's not easy to get a novel published in today's climate but you can definitely maximise your chances by doing certain things and avoiding others. The very first tip is to START RIGHT NOW! If you don't, life will pass you by and it could be too late. Recently, I had a student who came to me for advice on writing her first novel. She is in her early sixties (although she looks much younger) and told me that she had always wanted to write. But instead, she married young and had two beautiful daughters now grown up. She went on to have two more marriages and then married her third husband. The two of them lived busy lives pursuing their own careers until one day she had an unexpected accident and broke her neck. Miraculously, she survived, although it was hit and miss as to whether she would end up in a wheelchair.

'When I came round from the operation and the surgeon said that, against most odds, I would walk again, I decided to do two things,' she told me. *'The first was to buy a house in France, which I'd always dreamed of doing. And the second was to write a novel, which is why I am here.'*

We might not all be able to buy a house in France! But you don't need any money to write a novel. Apart, perhaps, from the cover price of this book.

I hope it helps – and I'd love to hear from you after you've read it.

Good luck!

Sophie King

www.sophieking.info

1

Are You Ready to Commit?

Do you have time to have another baby? Can you squeeze in enough time in your already busy day, to nurture ideas while holding down a busy job? (Tip: write them down in your Ideas book, even though the children are screaming for your attention.) And – this is the big one – do you have time to sit down and write every day for anything from four months to over a year?

Put off already? Then you might want to think again about how serious you really are as a writer. There are a lot of people who like the idea of having a book published. There are also those 'know-alls' who are convinced they could do a better job than many of those who succeed in getting on the shelves. But there are also the 'one day' writers. In other words, those who will definitely write a book one day when the children are older or when they retire or when they 'have more time'.

But if you are a real writer, you will have no choice. The ideas will keep flooding into your head. They will knock on your mind when you are trying to do the normal stuff in life. They won't leave you alone and in fact they might make you feel quite ratty until you sit down and start writing. Then it's like a magic drug. You instantly feel better. And if you continue, a strange thing will happen. It becomes easier to sit down and carry on where you left off.

‘ *I've always wanted to write a novel but I wanted children too. I told myself I would start writing when my third went to school. But then I found I was pregnant again! I used my maternity leave to start my novel and after my fourth son was born, I wrote when he was asleep even though I was tired. That novel didn't get accepted but at least I finished it – which made me realise I could write another. By then, my 'baby' had gone to playgroup so I had an extra two hours a day. He's still there and I'm still writing. The house isn't as tidy as it could be because of my novel which is now almost finished. Sometimes my husband understands and sometimes he doesn't. But I know that if I hadn't done this, I would always have felt something was lacking in my life.* ’

Anon.

WRITING EVERY DAY

OK. So you definitely think you want to write a book and my slightly harsh opening paragraphs haven't put you off. You've actually made a start and have written a page or two or even a first chapter. But then comes another hurdle. Try as you have, you simply haven't been able to make time for any more. And somehow, a few weeks or even a few months have gone by and now you are sitting at your desk again – or lolling on the sofa with your laptop – but you've lost the thread. And the pages that you've already written and seemed enthralling at the time of writing, now don't seem any good.

There's a reason for this. It's probably because you had that break. When you're reading a book and you – for whatever reason – have to stop reading it every day for a week or more, it doesn't seem so gripping, does it? You've stopped caring about the character's dilemma or what will happen next because you haven't been paying enough attention. You haven't been turning the pages every day and, as a result, you've left the fantasy world which that novel created for you. So it's going to take time to get back into it again.

It's exactly the same when it comes to writing a novel, instead of just reading it. If you step outside the world of your characters and become engaged in the so-called 'real' world, you lose that 'pull' of the land you have created on screen or on paper.

That's all very well, you say. But you have to earn a living. You have to look after the baby. You have to care for your elderly mother. Yet the good news is that you can still do all this. I'm not suggesting you drop all your responsibilities. But you have to – if you're going to be serious about this – squeeze an extra 15 minutes or ideally an hour into your day so you can write.

This might mean getting up an hour earlier. Or going to bed an hour later – and using that time to write. It could be giving up your lunch hour and writing on your laptop with a sandwich at your side instead. It might even be getting a DVD for the kids for an hour or so. But the most important thing is that you treat it like cleaning your teeth, teenage-style. It needs to be done once a day.

> ❛ *DO write little and often – every day if you can, even just for a few minutes or a few hundred words. I find Dr Wicked's writing lab very good for that: it makes you write against the clock in whatever short time period you have free. http://lab.drwicked.com/ writeordie.html – but DON'T FORGET it's a learning process. You can only learn to write fiction by doing it, rather like an*

apprentice carpenter will only learn his craft by working with wood. There's a theory that you only master something – whether it's music, sport or writing – after putting in ten thousand hours of work. OK, some writers have a gift that bypasses the apprenticeship, but for the rest of us, it's about putting the hours in. That also has the advantage of giving you time to explore what you want to write – theme, genre, voice – so that when the publisher or agent calls, you have more than one book and idea to offer them!

Kate Harrison, author of seven novels including
The Secret Shopper's Revenge and *The Secret Shopper Unwrapped.*

FINDING YOUR BEST WRITING TIME

This is something which took me a while to work out. Depending on your own personality, there are certain times of the day when you write better than others. Of course, you may not have the luxury of choosing when you are going to write. It could be that, as we've already discussed, there may only be one or even no opportunities in your already packed schedule. But think again. If you find that doesn't work, how about lunchtime? Some people actually need the stimulus of a morning to get their creative juices flowing.

Personally speaking, I'm a morning person. I write best when I have got my nearest and dearest up; walked the dog; had breakfast and then cleared away. But if I start to do the housework or make that phone call, I'm doomed. Somehow that slightly distant feeling which remains from a night's sleep has gone. And that in turn affects the way I write. It's just not so fresh.

The good news, however, is that you can teach yourself to write at a different time from the one that you think you write best at. Some years ago now, I found myself on my own with one child after a long marriage. Suddenly I had to go out to work instead of being freelance. I panicked so much about my bank account that I found myself taking on writing jobs outside the home for four days a week. 'How will you have time to write?' asked a horrified novelist friend.

I didn't know. But I also knew that on the days when I didn't write (because I was so tired and busy with my teenager), I felt worse than ever. So although I'd always told myself I couldn't write at night, I made myself sit down. And then I discovered a strange thing. I got a second wind. Sometimes my writing seemed different at that time of the day but it still seemed to work. In fact, it gave me greater insight into my characters because I'd been out all day, seeing different people.

As well as discovering my 'hidden night owl', I also began writing during my lunch hour. And I always, always, take my laptop with me on train journeys. In fact, I'm writing this chapter on the way to Wales where I'm teaching a course for Writers' Holiday. Never waste a moment! I've already got an idea for my next chapter from the two people talking next to me, but more of that in Chapter 7 on characterisation.

You could have the opposite problem. I have friends who have so much time that they can't pin themselves down to write. There will always be time later on in the day – until suddenly it's bedtime. Oh well, there's tomorrow...and then the next day!

Now this is when I would suggest using that morning time. Treat it like a date with yourself. Put it in your diary. And if the dentist wants you to come before 11am, tell him/her you're working. Don't let anyone else get in your way. You've earned this time for yourself. So use it!

YES – WRITING *IS* WORKING!

'I knew you were in so I thought you might fancy a coffee!'

How often have you found a neighbour or friend on your doorstep with this well-meaning remark? There's only one reply. 'I'm working, thanks. Can we make it later?'

I know what you're thinking. How can you really be working if you're unpublished yet? But if you don't start seeing your book as work and taking it seriously, how can you expect other people to do so?

It's a bit trickier, however, if it's a Sunday morning and your husband wants you to go to the pub or you've planned to take the kids out. And this is where a certain compromise needs to be reached. I'm not suggesting that you step apart from family life, But nor does this mean you can never have time to yourself. It's up to you to work out the details if you are really going to give yourself a fair crack at writing.

I have to say here that it helps if you have understanding family and/or an understanding partner who doesn't accuse you of neglecting everyone if you sneak off for a tête-à-tête with your hero. But I do feel honour-bound to point out that, unfortunately, some men (and women) feel threatened by a partner who writes. They don't always like it if someone does something away from them. And they might just be scared that they will end up on the page. I'm not going to say what you should do because this is too personal for both you and me. But if you want my opinion, a partner who really loves you and understands your ambition, will understand.

On the other hand, a boss might not! One famous novelist friend of mine recalls how she started writing her first novel under the desk at work for an advertising agency. After a number of warnings, she was asked to leave. The irony is that although she put the novel that got her into trouble in a drawer for a year, her husband persuaded her to send it to a publisher and the rest is history!

WRITERS' BLOCK

So you've managed to make that spare time to write. Well done! But now you're sitting there in front of your laptop or with a piece of paper in front of you and the words won't come! The first thing is not to panic. It happens – and to lots of established writers. But there's a great way (almost foolproof) of getting round this. It works like this. Write down – right now – whatever comes into your head. It doesn't matter if it's a shopping list. Or it could be 'Someone's told me to write and I don't know what to put down'. Just write for a total of five minutes. Set your alarm clock or the kitchen timer. Make your hand move across the page and don't allow yourself to stop.

When you've finished, read what you've just written. You might be surprised. Sometimes people come out with thoughts and ideas that are hidden deep inside that they didn't know they had. And this can be a great way of thinking up a storyline.

When I run my writers' groups, I always ask students to start with flash fiction. 'Write whatever comes into your head,' I say.

Here is an example that one of my students has kindly let me use.

> 'Isn't it funny how you turn to friends you haven't spoken to for ages, when you're in trouble? The other day I rang my sister-in-law. We haven't talked for years. But she could tell from the tone in my voice that I needed to talk. So we did. Now I wonder why we haven't done more of that.'

This was a short piece as you can see. It happened to be true – even though flash fiction can be entirely fictitious. And it gave my student an idea for her novel. We called the idea a 'plot pusher' because it pushed the plot along by making one of her characters get in touch with a teacher whom she hadn't seen for a long time. This led to another event and then another. . .

Sometimes, flash fiction is just a list of words that don't seem to have any connection. Here's another example, again from one of my students.

> Dark. Warm. Happy to be alone. Hot water bottle. Furry. Bed. Curled up. Sprawled on both sides. Linen. Launderette. Change. An old newspaper lying on the side.

My student wasn't sure why this image had come into her head because she hadn't been to a launderette for years! But it did make her feel that she ought to send her heroine to one.

And another way of beating writers' block. . .
Some students find it hard to write about whatever comes into their head. So try opening a magazine and pick a picture that jumps out at you. It might be a glossy ad or it could be an

illustration for a feature. Now use that as a trigger for 'flash fiction'. Tell yourself that you simply have to write something about it. It's all about commitment. And you might be surprised at what comes out. I often use a picture showing lots of different hands reaching out for each other. I'm amazed at how many different pieces of writing I've had from students, all of whom have interpreted it in different ways.

If this doesn't work for you, try closing your eyes and listen to the sounds around you. Write them down. Do the same for smells.

Make a list of these smells and sounds and then write five lines, incorporating them. Again, this might give you ideas or it could have just started your hand to write – which is exactly the purpose of the whole exercise.

Alternatively, write the outline of a favourite fairy tale. Or a drama you've seen on TV. Or a story you've read. Ask yourself how you might have written it differently. Change one or two of the main facts and see what you come up with. We're beginning to encroach here on my next chapter on Ideas but the main point is that you now have some tools to get that hand moving. It's all part of that commitment to writing your first novel!

And one more!
Try writing in a different place. Experiment! It's amazing what a different location can do in terms of inspiration, especially if it means you can sit and 'people watch'. Here's a list of not-so-obvious places that you might be able to write in.

◆ Hospital car park.
◆ Coffee shop in a busy department store.

- ◆ Park bench.
- ◆ Your car in a multi-storey car park.
- ◆ On a beach in winter.
- ◆ A friend's study (swap his/hers with yours).
- ◆ Someone else's bedroom (this could include your children's).

TIP

You might also be able to shift writers' block by listening to music at the same time. However, some writers (including myself) can't bear any kind of noise when writing!

WRITING TOOLS

Personally speaking, I write best on my laptop. In fact, I can't write very well on paper any more. But that's because I've been using my keyboard for years now thanks to my original training as a journalist. I find it faster – my fingers fly across the letters in a way they couldn't if I wrote on paper and that means my pace is more immediate and I can get my ideas out without forgetting them.

The golden rule about writing on a keyboard is to always, always, back up. This means saving your work somewhere else apart from your computer in case it breaks or is stolen. One tip is to email yourself with your novel file. You should then be able to access this from another computer if something happens to yours. I do this – and I also email it to my daughter with the words DO NOT READ! Alternatively, you could save it to a memory stick, although you need to make sure you don't lose it.

However, I have friends at the top of the Bestseller lists who can only write on paper. They then write it up afterwards. Some people pay others to type it up for them, although obviously this is going to cost. However – and forgive me if this sounds basic – an agent and publisher won't consider a piece if it isn't typed.

Never, ever, edit or read through your work on screen. You will miss things. Trust me on this. Far better to print out each chapter and then read it through. Read it out loud if you can. That way you will see if a comma should be a full stop (if you pause for a second, it's a comma but any longer and it's probably a full stop or a semi colon). Reading it out loud will also help you to spot a character whose internal thought goes on too much (a page or more) or where there isn't enough action (I aim for one to two main events per chapter), or if there isn't enough dialogue (this should start on the first page). I'll be giving you more tips on these guidelines later on!

ARE YOU SITTING COMFORTABLY?

Finding the right place to write your novel makes a huge difference. It's like wearing the right clothes to an interview. If you feel comfortable, it will come across in your own attitude and also in your writing.

It helps if you have your own room to write in, but don't panic if you don't. Try to sort out a corner of a room which is yours for writing. If you have to do different types of writing such as office reports or journalism or writing letters, try to do it in a different spot. The first one should be yours for writing that novel.

Is your chair comfortable? Check it's the right height for your desk. Is there too much noise around you? If so, you may need to move. Many writers have sheds at the bottom of their garden (I have a summer house where I write when it's warm enough). Several writers use the library. Jane Green, whom I visited one year in her home in Westport, writes in the library every day. The library can be a good cut off and you can treat it like an office. No one can bother you there and there are no phones to answer.

If you have a laptop rather than a large computer that can't be moved, try moving it round to different places in the house and see if it stimulates your writing. I sometimes write on my dining room table in the winter or in the front room. But I try to avoid my work study because it's full of papers and it's bang next to my son's noisy bedroom!

HOW DO YOU KNOW IT'S NOT A WASTE OF TIME?

Ah! Now this is a question that haunts many writers – often before they start! A novel requires months if not years of dedication. Supposing it doesn't get published? Isn't that a waste of time?

The answer is simple. Not if you're a real writer. If you are, you will write if no one pays you. In fact, you'd pay someone to LET you write. Actually, this is a very good test to check that you're doing the right thing – rather like the princess and the pea story! A real writer will feel bruised if rejected but will have to carry on and on, even if nothing ever happens.

The good news is that these years spent writing novels that may not be published are actually excellent preparation for writing THE novel that does make it in the end. I myself wrote ten novels over ten years until the eleventh, *The School Run*, was published by

Hodder & Stoughton. I call it my self-imposed apprenticeship. During those ten novels, I learned to craft characters; work out which ideas would be sustainable for a novel; write authentic dialogue; and create a plot which kept the reader turning the pages.

And that's exactly what we're going to do in the rest of this book! So keep writing...

HOW TO GIVE YOURSELF MORE TIME WRITING EACH DAY

In my introduction, I talked about 'things' that can get in the way when you're trying to write a novel. Some of these are (hopefully) wonderful distractions such as a partner and/or children that you wouldn't be without. But it is still possible to have them and make an extra half an hour a day in order to write.

Here are some ideas to give you more writing time:

◆ Do a swap with a friend; you have her children for a certain amount of time and then she has yours.

◆ Negotiate 'writing time' with your partner so he gives you time by having the children or just leaving you in peace. Then you do the same while he does 'his thing'.

◆ If you have a busy job that doesn't give you much time, try writing in your lunch hour. Find a library or even a bench if the weather is fine. If you stay in the office to write, someone is bound to interrupt you.

◆ Use your holiday leave wisely. Take a day off a month and call it your writing day.

♦ Try getting up half an hour earlier to write. Do it in your
  dressing gown. Once you start having a shower, getting dressed
  or doing housework, you'll lose that time to write.

♦ Go to bed half an hour later and use that time to start your
  novel. You might feel you are tired but some writers get over that
  and have a second wind. (See the section on Best Writing Time.)

♦ If you have children, let them lie in on high days and holidays.
  Use that time to write while they are asleep (if you're not at
  work) and then you can be with them for the rest of the day
  when they wake – after having written a chapter!

♦ Give up a gym class or a favourite television programme and
  use that as writing time.

Warning!

When I started writing my novels (the ones that weren't
published), an older and wiser writing friend told me that novels
could sometimes break up marriages. 'Husbands can feel
threatened by their wives' stories,' she told me. 'And not all
husbands like being left alone in the sitting room while their wives
or partners are upstairs, pounding the word processor.'

I'm not going to comment on my own experiences as that
wouldn't be fair. But let's just say that I have seen this situation
happen with other writers. So be aware of it. And try to get the
balance right!

SUMMARY

♦ You need to be committed to write a novel. You might need to
  make sacrifices. But at least you will have been true to yourself.

After all, you'll have followed that little voice inside yourself that says 'Give it a go!'

- Little and often is better than nothing at all. Five minutes a day helps you keep the plot in your head more than an hour a week.

- Use the right tools. Try working on a word processor. And also with a pen. Experiment with different types of keyboards and different pens.

- Write in a place where you feel comfortable. If you're at ease, your writing will flow better.

- Have faith in yourself. Tell yourself that you CAN do this.

- Find your best writing time. You might find that you are fresher in the morning. But you might also discover that you get a second wind in the evening.

❛ *You hear a lot of writers saying they write a thousand words a day, which sounds daunting. I like smaller targets (my current target is one hundred words – but I try and do that ten or more times each day! Try a page a day. If you write a page a day for a year, you've got your first draft.* ❜

Sue Moorcroft, *Love Writing – How to Make Money Writing Romantic or Erotic Fiction; Starting Over; Family Matters; Uphill all the Way; Between Two Worlds; A Place to Call Home.*

2

A Novel Idea!

HOW TO THINK OF THAT WINNING IDEA

What kinds of books are publishers looking for at the moment? It's a question that comes up time and time again at talks. And there's usually one answer. The publisher (and agent) will know what they want when they see it! How annoying is that?

But you can also see what they mean. It's a bit like falling in love. You might think you are looking for a tall Mr Right with a sports car and a mother who loves you. But then you go and fall for someone who's a nose shorter than you with a motorbike and a mother who loathes you at first sight. But somehow, you just know instinctively, that this is the man for you!

Some publishers and agents will tell you that certain genres are doing well in the current market. At the time of writing, historicals and crime are being 'well-received', although contemporary romantic comedy is as difficult to crack as ever.

However, if you decide to change your writing and suddenly switch from sci-fi, which is your real passion, to historicals (even though you know nothing of life before 1979), you could be in trouble. And not because you don't know the period, because this is something you can research. No, it's because your heart won't really be in it. It will be hankering after little green men instead. And if you're not passionate about your writing, the chances are that your would-be publisher and agent (let alone the reader), won't be either.

In my view, it's the idea that counts rather than the genre. If you come up with a cracking good idea that no one has thought of before or which is a really original take on an idea which has been done, you stand a good chance of being moved from the 'Might Just be Possible' slush pile to the 'Might be Possible' pile.

Yes, that's me!

I believe that if you can find an idea for a novel that others will identify with, you're on to a winner. I call this the 'Yes, that's me!' factor. It's when readers really believe that the heroine is just like them or how they would like to be – or that she is like someone else she knows.

Why is this important? It's because it makes the book believable. For instance, readers love Sophie Kinsella's shopaholic books because they might be guilty of spending too much money themselves sometimes – or they know someone who does. They also like the fact that the heroine is warm and funny.

TRICKS AND TIPS ON HOW TO FIND A NOVEL IDEA

So how do you find that wonderful idea which will make your novel stand out in the slush pile?

Here are tried and tested techniques which have worked for me and several other writers I know.

Real life

Some of the best ideas for novels come from events which really happened. It might be a great aunt who leaves you a cottage in the Lake District that you never knew about before. It might be a woman who didn't think she could have children and then has a baby, after her husband had left her. (And she isn't sure if it's his child or the man with whom she had a 'comfort stand' when he went.) Or it might be the girl who discovered that her aunt was really her mother.

All these stories above are true. But I'm not suggesting that you reproduce them faithfully like a real-life magazine article. If you do that, you could leave yourself open to a libel action or hurt someone.

However, you could take part of that story and add a layer or two of fiction. For instance, the woman who had the baby might find out that she was having twins; and that it was medically possible that one baby might be her husband's and the other, a handsome stranger's. The story could centre on those two children growing up and their quest later on in life to find their real father.

The aunt who left a cottage in the Lake District could be changed to an uncle who left a villa in Italy – together with the covenant that the niece who inherited it had to also look after the elderly neighbour next door. Maybe – and I'm letting my imagination run riot on this one – the neighbour was an elderly woman who had had a love affair with the uncle who had never married. And maybe – this is a big leap here! – the elderly female neighbour might turn out to be an aunt. (In other words, she gave birth to the niece's mother whom everyone thought was adopted.)

You'll see that I've combined two ideas here from the real-life scenarios that I've outlined above. This is because a combination of two or more real-life ideas can create a very energetic plot in fiction.

EXERCISE

Of course, some people have more exciting lives than others. You might feel that nothing much has happened to you. But you could be surprised. I often get students saying this to me and then, when I ask them some questions, they suddenly think of something.

If you need some prompts, ask yourself the following questions:

◆ What big surprises have you had in life? (These could be nice surprises or shocks.)
◆ Have you ever lost something important?
◆ Have you found something special?
◆ If you were at the end of your life and someone asked you which events stood out in your mind, what would you say right now?
◆ Have you come across any surprising coincidences in life?
◆ What has your happiest time been – and why?
◆ What has your darkest time been – and why?
◆ List all the important people in your life and then think about how you met them.

I bet that by now, you'll have thought of some big events in your life. These might or might not make a story but it will get you thinking ■

EXERCISE

This exercise will also help you to think of real-life events that could be put into fiction. If you're using this book as a text book in a classroom or in a writing group, you could try it in pairs. Otherwise do it on your own.

Write down at least one thing (but preferably two or three) which has happened to you or someone you know. It needs to be the sort of thing where you might ring up a friend and say 'You'll never guess what happened!'.

If you're doing this in pairs, you each have a minute to tell each other about something amazing that happened and then you swap over. The idea is that you tell the rest of the class about your partner's amazing 'thing' because writers need to listen carefully as well as natter! ▇

Here are some examples of incredible happenings that have come from previous students (with their permission).

Woman about to get married, discovers that the old newspaper her mother used years ago, to line her underwear drawer, had a picture of her future husband when he played for the local football team. (This was before she met him.)

Mother starts school run in new area and discovers that one of the other mothers on the run was a friend of hers from her own school at the other end of the country.

Husband loses his wife when she gives birth and brings up twins on his own.

Mother-in-law loses key down a drain in the road and then two hours later, discovers that the council have started to dig up the road for 'maintenance'. She gets them to lift the drain cover and find her key.

All these stories are true but only two might make a novel. Can you guess which ones?

Let's take the first one about the bride and the football player. My feeling is that this wouldn't be enough to base an entire novel on. This is because it relies for impact on one incident – discovering the picture. However, it could be what I call a 'plot-pusher'. In other words, an event which moves a plot along in a longer piece. It's a discovery which could make the bride feel that fate had a hand in her relationship with this man. And that in itself might be enough to make her overcome her doubts and get married. However, afterwards, she might feel she's made a terrible mistake. And then something else happens.

Or we could use it as another kind of plot-pusher. The bride finds the picture. The face is unmistakeably that of her future fiancé. But he has another name – a name which he has never disclosed to her. And that might make her realise he has a secret past.

Isn't it interesting how the same idea can make a novel go in two different directions?

There are some ideas which are actually perfect short stories. But the writer tries to make them into a novel and so they don't work. This is usually because the idea doesn't have the potential to stretch into a longer story which goes on for 100,000 words plus. This kind of idea needs branch shoots. It needs possibilities which could open up into several plot-pushers.

I think that the bride and the picture might make a short story as well as being a plot-pusher within a longer piece. The twist at the end could be that she is the football player in an all-girls team. However, you'd have to be careful when writing the story not to use the word 'he' when referring to the player. Instead, you could write it so as to fool the reader into assuming it's a man.

This isn't a book on how to write short stories. If you want that, you need to read my *How to Write Short Stories and Get Published*. However, it is important to work out which ideas make novels naturally and which are actually short stories in disguise.

Let's take the next idea about the mother who starts a new school run and finds an old school friend. This happened to me and was partly what helped me think of the idea for my first novel *The School Run*. It could make a short story with a feel-good flavour. Perhaps the mothers didn't actually like each other and are now naturally apprehensive about meeting up again. However, their daughters become good friends, so forcing the mothers together, and they discover they have more in common now they are adults, than when they were children.

But it could also, as my book shows, become a novel – because it has scope for expansion. In *The School Run*, I took seven characters each on the same route to school. My mothers were just two of them and in fact, I didn't make them old school friends. I just made them good friends. Everyone else on the run were very different characters, which was important for the mix. But the main point is that the whole idea of taking the children to school is something which many of us deal with every day of our lives. And even if we don't have kids to take, we might get caught up in the school run. Consequently, it struck what I call the 'Yes, that's me!' chord. In other words, it was recognisable by other people. It was a subject that they were familiar with so they felt on safe ground. And yet it was intriguing because they wanted to know what would happen to each of those characters.

The husband who loses his wife idea (also true) and brings up twin daughters, is a sombre one. There's no getting away from that. And on the whole, short stories need to be able to wrap up a problem in anything from 800–1800 words. That might be tricky with such a sad story. Does it have to be sad? Not, I think, if you have the space to introduce some humour. If I was a betting woman, which

I'm not, I'd say this might make a novel. It has lots of possibilities which will take the reader over the course of several months if not years. How does dad manage to bring up babies, let alone toddlers? Will he meet a mother from the children's school who is conveniently on her own? Supposing the grandparents begin to interfere in the children's upbringing? What happens if the children find out that their mother died because their father was driving the family car too fast? This isn't actually what happened in the real story but it might... It has all the potential to be a tear jerker. In fact, I can see it on screen, which is another test. If you can picture your story on film and lasting more than a few minutes, you may have the makings of a novel.

Now on to the key and drain story. Again this happened to me! Honestly. And although I love to tell this tale, I don't think it is long enough to make into a novel. However, it could be a plot-pusher. Heroine in a flap, drops key and sexy council worker finds it in drain. He's not the kind of man she was looking for and yet there's a certain charm in his raffish behaviour. Could it make a short story? Possibly, although I think it might be a short story if we can think of a twist. Over to you.

Do you see what I'm getting at? Certain ideas have definite possibilities for novels because they have potential to go on and cover more problems and branch out into even more dilemmas. But some are cameo scenes within a novel and others would be more suited as a short story.

Getting your idea right is absolutely essential if your first novel is going to succeed. So please read this chapter again and then have a go at the exercise at the end of the chapter.

Are you re-hashing old themes?

An idea, as we've already discussed, needs that X factor. That Wow element which makes everyone sit up and think 'That's different! Why didn't I think of that before?'

So why is it that new writers – and some old ones too – constantly come up with themes that have been done before and still expect publishers and agents to pick them up?

Here are some well-worn themes:

- School reunions.
- Singles holidays.
- Adoption stories.
- Dotty heroines seeking Mr Right.

Stop! Before you throw your manuscript in the bin, this doesn't mean that you can't write a novel with these themes. But you will need to twist it a different way so that they suddenly get a facelift. What if the school reunion involved a celebrity who was found dead at the end of the reunion lunch?

Supposing the singles holiday was more about the reps than the guests?

What if you told the adoption story from the point of view of three people involved, e.g. the natural mother; the adoptive mother; the child?

Supposing you have three desperate bachelors looking for Miss Right?

When my children were young, they adored Babette Cole's books. She turns traditional fairy tales around so, instead of Cinderella, she has a Prince Cinders with stepbrothers instead of stepsisters. This is the kind of unusual idea treatment which will make an idea stand out and have that X factor.

Write about what you know

I'm a great believer in writing about what you know. I think it makes a novel much more realistic and will convince the reader that you understand the world you are describing. My background is in journalism so I usually have a journalist in my novels. I have also brought up three lively children and I've got divorced and re-married. Again, I write about these themes, although I didn't until they happened to me because I wouldn't have felt qualified to write it. My mother died young (at about my age), so I feel I can write about the loss of a mother too. But I've read writers who have written about all these things without actually having experienced those emotions personally. They may have interviewed people to whom they have happened but it's not the same, is it? And I think that comes through in the writing.

So my advice is to write about what you know. By all means do your research (see Chapter 6), but remember it's not a substitute for the real thing.

EXERCISE

Take another look at the real-life idea you came up with. Write a brief story outline based on this idea.

Now write down any other idea you have for a novel. Again, write a brief story outline. Ask yourself if it has the potential to stretch out for a whole book. Is it interesting enough? Is it too predictable? Read the outline to a friend or someone who isn't in your writing group, and ask if they would read a book like this. If not, why?

Can you sum up your idea in one sentence? If it's a Wow idea, you should be able to.

Think of your novel as a stage

In order for a novel to have lots of things going on, you need to set it in a place or situation where there is the potential for various events to happen – and for all kinds of different characters to pop up.

Here are some examples:

- A gym.
- Dog training classes.
- A dress shop.
- A hotel.
- A holiday group.
- A dancing class/group.
- An amateur dramatics company.
- A quiz evening.

Each one of these ideas is going to have a mixture of personalities and the possibility of arguments and tension. We need this to make the story come alive and for the reader to turn the page in order to see what happens.

For example, the gym might have a new class in spinning – that's an exercise where you do bike-based exercises. One of the new members might know someone else's husband; perhaps they were boyfriend and girlfriend as teenagers. This fact might not come out until halfway through the course. Perhaps the woman running the course is having problems with her teenage son. Maybe there's one male member of the class who is constantly being 'chased' by someone else in the group. Already, we're getting the feel for a plot that could run and run (preferably on one of the gym machines).

Here are some other ways you could develop from the list above. Try adding some of your own and see if it makes you think of different ways in which a potential novel could develop.

Dog training classes. The different relationships amongst the owners of the various dogs and how this changes from week to week.

A dress shop. Stories behind the different customers and staff. Or you could look at the clothes themselves and where they go to when they are bought.

A hotel. The stories behind the guests and staff. Or a story about the building itself and what has happened to it over the years.

A holiday group. The backstories to the travellers (in other words, what has been happening in their lives until now) and then how the holiday changes them.

A dancing class/group. How dancing could inspire the different characters to change and tackle problems in their lives. For instance, one man might join a Salsa group because his wife is in a wheelchair and he is desperate to dance again.

An amateur dramatics company. The ups and downs of the very different characters in a play. Can they get to the final rehearsal without a showdown?

A quiz evening. Rivalry between different teams. What happens if the quiz master is challenged on a question?

All of this could make for a novel with lots going on!

Use magazines and newspapers as triggers for ideas

Hands up those of you who read the local paper. If you don't, shame on you! Too many people dismiss what they see as 'the local rag' without opening it and finding some great stories which could then, with a bit of imagination, be transformed into a novel idea.

Here are some stories from my local paper which could make a great tale.

Unemployed teenager finds Roman coins in neighbour's back garden. The teenager offered to help his elderly neighbour to dismantle the garden shed. Underneath it, they found a stash of old coins which turned out to be worth quite a bit.

Now this is the true story. But how could we make it into a novel? I don't know what happened to the coins but we could imagine some scenarios. Supposing the elderly neighbour insisted on sharing his good fortune with the unemployed teenager and that together, they set up a business offering to garden for other people.

That's quite an interesting idea but I don't know that it has the length and the substance to make a long novel. However, it

MIGHT make a historical if we approach it from a different angle. Supposing the scene where the teenager and the elderly neighbour find the coins is a prologue. Then we go into a long flashback (consisting of most of the novel) where we follow the history of the coins. We could start in Roman times and tell the story of the men and women who used them. Then we could follow the coins and their owners through the centuries until we come to the present day.

Here's another idea, this time, from a magazine feature about three women who have started their lives all over again after some kind of a catastrophe. One woman lost her leg in a train crash; another lost all her money when her new husband gambled it away; and a third lost both her husband and her son in a motorway crash.

All three scenarios are pretty depressing at first sight. In reality, each of those women found something to help them cope with the after-effects. I'm not going to say they got over their tragedies because I'm not sure that's possible but, just like literary heroines, they were able to summon up courage to live with what had happened to them.

In fact, this kind of plot is often known as triumph over tragedy. It is a great way of showing that people are made of amazingly strong stuff and that we can overcome the odds. Readers love stories like this, whether they're real or not. Just think of Barbara Taylor Bradford's wonderful novel *Woman of Substance*, which was about a very feisty heroine who survived the odds that life threw at her.

You could use the magazine idea to create three strong women who had had similar experiences. If I was writing a novel like this, I would have a flashback so that the reader could learn to identify with the heroines before the tragedies. In this way, they will feel more for them when those tragedies happened. Then I would follow the stories of my imaginary heroines and show how they managed to claw their way back up. Of course, they would need a few set-backs on the way or else it would be too easy, but that would be part of the story.

EXERCISE

Pick six articles from newspapers and magazines. See if they suggest any novel ideas to you. If you belong to a writing group, do this exercise round the table. You might be surprised at what you come up with ■

TIP

Always buy the local paper if you're on holiday or even away for the day. You'll be surprised at what you might find! For instance, I recently bought a local paper in the Lake District and there was a story about a dog who had found his way home after ten years. That might make a novel on how a family had changed during that time.

Read the classified ads too!

The 'For Sale' sign can be a great source of ideas for novels (and short stories too). Look through the classifieds every week and see if something catches your eye.

Here are some examples that I have found:

Ad: *100 piece jigsaw. Six pieces missing.*

Novel idea: *a story about those six pieces and where each one of them ended up. Or a story about a woman who was obsessed with jigsaws.*

Ad: *Victorian desk. Drawer won't open.*
Novel idea: *a story about the owners of the desk in the past and why the drawer won't open.*

EXERCISE

Find three classified ads in your local paper. See if you can think of a novel idea ▧

Picture it!

Magazine pictures can also give you ideas for novel plots. (We're also going to be using magazine pictures for settings, but that's later on.)

For example, I recently found a picture of a mountain with a small figure on the top. That made me wonder if I could write a novel about a woman who was scared of heights but made herself go on a mountain challenge for charity. The novel could consist of some flashbacks on why she was scared of heights, intermingled with the physical demands of the climb and the people she met on her journey.

EXERCISE

Cut out ten pictures from magazines and see if they suggest any ideas to you. I recently did this with a class of students I teach. This is what they came up with.

Picture of a garden = trigger for a novel about a garden through the ages and its different owners.

Picture of the coastline in the north east = trigger for a novel about a woman who moves to a different part of the country.

Picture of a summer house = trigger for a novel about a woman who moves into the garden shed to escape from her family. (This caused a great deal of humour!) It was suggested that the novel was set over one week as it might be practically difficult for her to live there any longer■

TIP

Don't throw out all the Sunday supplements. Cut out pictures that look interesting and laminate them for future use.

Agony aunt pages

These are also a fantastic way to think of a good book. It's also a good excuse to read as many 'Dear Marge' letters as possible. Here are some examples, taken from a selection of newspapers and magazines.

- A woman who secretly fancies her future husband's brother.
- A man who doesn't get on with his boss.
- A bachelor who is about to marry a woman with four children.

Each one of those might make a novel in its own right. The woman who fancies her future husband's brother might decide that she has to put such thoughts out of her mind. He admits he feels the same for her, before the marriage, so he emigrates to

Australia to put temptation out of reach. But years later, when her own marriage has broken up, she tries to trace him.

A man who doesn't get on with his boss might form a plot-pusher. It might not be the basis for an entire novel because I'm not sure that the story is strong enough. But it could certainly be a scene in a longer book.

A bachelor who is about to marry a woman with four children could be a very funny book – if not a film. He's going to come across all kinds of problems, isn't he? And there will also need to be some warm moments too.

EXERCISE

Write a letter to an imaginary agony aunt. You could use one of your problems (you must have some!) or a problem that a friend has got.

If you are doing this in a class, swap it with a neighbour and answer each other's problems. If you are doing this on your own, pretend you are the agony aunt and answer your own. Or get someone in the family to act as agony aunt.

You might come up with some great novel ideas ■

Television and radio

Recently, I told one of my students (who happens to be in prison where I am currently writer in residence), that I don't have much time to watch television. He gave me a sad look before proceeding to tell me off. I would, he said, get some great ideas for plots if I sat down and watched a soap opera or a drama series.

So I tried it. And he was right. It was a lesson to me that relaxing in front of the television can actually be 'homework'!

Personally, I listen to the radio a lot. And that gives me ideas too. I often listen to stations that I've never heard of, for variety. It's worth trying.

TIP

Always keep a pad of paper and pencil with you at all times, even next to the bed. When you think of an idea, write it down or you'll forget it. Honestly!

Keep your eyes and ears open

Always listen out for other people's conversations (providing it doesn't get you into trouble!). Use it as an excuse to sit in a coffee shop and observe what is going on. When you're on a train or a bus, listen to what the man, woman or child is saying either on the mobile or to each other.

STILL NOT SURE IF YOUR IDEA WILL WORK?

Then ask yourself the following questions:

◆ Will it strike a chord with most readers?

◆ Is there scope for a series of action events?

◆ Is there a wide enough stage and setting so the reader doesn't get bored?

- Does your idea bring in enough characters for different readers to identify with?

- Has it been done several times before? If so, can you give it a different twist?

- Is it believable?

The answer needs to be 'yes' to most of these questions. If it's not, it might be an idea to think of another idea – or a variant of the first.

EXERCISE

Write down five different 'canvases' for a novel. For example, an amateur dramatic group; a garden centre; a school.

Now write down five different characters. For example, a headmistress; a down and out; a retired banker.

Then write down five different problems or difficulties in life. For example, moving house; losing something important; falling out with an aunt.

Cut out each idea so you have a total of fifteen strips of paper. Put the 'canvas' ideas into one jam jar. The 'character' ideas into a second jam jar. And the 'problems' in a third.

Take one strip of paper out of each jam jar and see what you come up with. For instance, you might have a headmistress who loses something important when she is in a play.

If that doesn't grab you, take another three pieces of paper and move them around so you come up with an idea that makes you think of a possible story for a novel

SUMMARY

- Find an idea that has lots of 'branches' so it will last for a whole novel with different sub-ideas for development.

- Write about what you know – but give it a twist.

- Learn to look at ideas from an unusual angle to find the 'wow' factor.

- Get ideas from:
  Real life
  Magazines/newspapers
  Classified ads
  Problem pages.

3

Finding Your Voice

There are certain phrases in 'how to write' books and workshops that come up again and again. One of the most common is 'Finding Your Voice'. Would-be authors are always being encouraged by authors and publishers to 'find their voice' if they are to be published. But what exactly does that mean?

Basically, your 'voice' is the way in which your book stands out from anyone else's. It might be the tone of your narrator which could be sarcastic or depressed or rambling or secretive or indeed anything that makes you think 'Goodness – that person is different'. For example, Fay Weldon's novels have a voice partly because the narrator is a main character with a very strong identity that's expressed through a sometimes tongue-in-cheek manner.

There are other ways too in which a novel has a voice. It could be an unusual way of treating a plot. *The Time Traveller's Wife* is, in my opinion, a good example. If you haven't read it, DO! It's about a woman whose husband lives at different times in different eras. The chronology leaps around all over the place so you have to keep on your toes. I loved it but I had to read the dates in the text carefully to know where I was. It was and still is a bestseller, which speaks volumes for the power of its voice.

Sometimes it's a combination of both: in other words, a tone of voice that wakes you up combined with an unusual way of looking at a plot. I personally found my voice when I discovered that what I liked doing best (alongside writing short stories) was to write novels from the point of view of at least four main characters. This is because I got bored with just concentrating on one heroine's problems. And I found that if I looked at the lives of three women and maybe one man, there was much more going on. Even better, I never got stuck on plot. (However, I do have to make sure that each character sounds and acts differently from the others; in other words, they need their own voice too. There's advice on how to do this in Chapter 7 on characterisation.)

I combined this with writing about contemporary dramatic situations such as parents who are terrified by the responsibility of bringing up children; mothers who leave their husbands or find themselves on their own; friends who fall out or meet up again; wedding guests who are going to be brought together in nine months' time.

This allowed me to bring in a wide cast of characters, which in turn provided lots of ideas for plot AND, according to the critics, gave my books a 'voice' of their own.

BUT HOW CAN YOU FIND YOURS?

I wish there was an easy answer. Some authors are lucky and find theirs immediately. Others, like me, take years to write different types of books before finding a tone or approach that they feel comfortable with. Suddenly, you'll realise that you can't stop writing. That the words just flow and that you feel passionate about what you're doing. You get a burning sensation down your back because you know – you just know – that you are writing something different.

I felt this with most of my novels but in particular, *The School Run* and also *The Wedding Party*. *The School Run* did this to me because very few authors, as far as I know, had written a novel about a subject which we are all aware of, whether we're apparent on the school run or just stuck behind a school-run car on the way to work.

And *The Wedding Party* did it to me because the characters are tackling tricky real-life issues which I've personally had experience of: divorce; prison (I'm writer in residence of an HMP); and re-marriage.

EXERCISE

Sit down with the phone off and write for five minutes without stopping or without thinking about what you're going to write. I don't care if you come up with a shopping list. I just want to know that your hand is moving across the page.

Afterwards, look at what you have written. You might discover – and I'm hoping you will – that you have produced something which is not like the kind of work you have written before. It might be a different subject that you didn't even know you had inside you. Or it could be a different style ▪

Here are some examples of flash fiction by my students and comments on how it helped them find their voices.

> Woke up. Felt sick. Remembered yesterday. Went back to sleep. Still there. Can't write. Must write . Makes me feel better. Should have put on washing machine before I came to class. So what?

It was the 'so what?' that helped this student. It helped her to think of a character with a 'so what?' attitude who had to change and become more sympathetic to others.

Why is it that socks always come out in ones? Why does my boss hate me? On my way to class tonight, I wondered if I could call in sick tomorrow. I know that's not right but my heart sinks when I think about work and it lifts up, right to the sky, when I imagine what I could be doing instead. Flying a kite. Catching a train to somewhere I have never been before. Going fishing.

This piece of flash fiction by a student inspired him to write a novel set over one day, about a man who takes a day off work and the accidents (not all bad!) that happen to him. Yet until he sat down to write the flash fiction in my class, he hadn't thought about the idea. I thought it was a good one because it taps into the child-like, free spirit inside us.

Read different types of books

If you don't normally read thrillers, go and buy one or browse in the library. Then, without thinking about a plot, make yourself write the first paragraph of a thriller. It might be from the point of view of the murderer or the victim or the bystander or the police. Just experiment. Does it feel exciting? If so, continue. This might be the kind of book that has been trying to get out.

Now do the same with historicals. Or romances. Or any other types of books that you don't normally have much to do with. It's a bit like going to a different place to find true love. In fact, finding your voice is very much like falling in love. It might hit you when you least expect it. But as soon as you find it, you wonder how you had managed without it for all these years because it is so right.

First and third person

Try writing in the first person if you usually write in the third. Or the third if you usually write in the first. Play around on the page. Make your narrative voice stronger so that someone is telling the tale. Or get inside one of your character's heads so you can pretend you are that person.

Here's an example of writing from inside a character's head from my novel *The Wedding Party*.

> Thank heavens. As soon as she walked into the chrome steel automatic rotating doors, Becky felt better. Here, at *Charisma* magazine, she was Becky Hastings, features editor instead of Becky Hughes, hopeless mother who couldn't cope without a nanny.
>
> Here – thank God – there was no one to shout at her. No one to scream when all she wanted to do was go to bed. No one who kept asking impossible questions like what keeps the clouds up in the sky and why don't they fall down. No one to throw temperatures of 103 like Daisy had last winter during Laura's day off and freak her out so she thought her daughter was dying only to be leaping up and down the next day.
>
> 'I love my children,' said Becky silently as though to convince herself. And she did. No one – least of all her mother who'd been desperate for her and Steve to get pregnant – had told her it would be like this, that's all.

Try writing with a friend

There's a trend at the moment for writing buddies. You see them everywhere. Two writers sitting at a table in a coffee shop, looking around and writing about the people they see. Some people write for moral support. But you can take this further. You write one paragraph about the people you see and then your friend writes another. Look at the different styles. Is there anything in them that might help you write in a different way? Could you write a book together with each one of you doing an alternate chapter?

> *Considering that writing is a very objective and creative process, it stands to reason that writing with someone else would be a disaster. In most creative partnerships – Gilbert & Sullivan, Lloyd Webber and Rice – one partner does one thing (lyrics) whilst the other does the other (score), but when you write together you are both pitching into the same process. The downside is that you can be intimidated – perhaps not using your full creative potential – and find yourself compromising when, alone, you would be more ruthless with passages or characters you weren't happy with. The up-side is that two heads are better than one – ideas get picked up and expanded. The imagination can be stretched when another person enters into the story going on in your head. Writing – especially these days when novels are harder and harder to get published – is a very lonely process, and it is very supportive to have someone working alongside you sharing your ups and downs . . . trouble is, you have to share the advance!!'*

Annie Ashworth, one half of the pen name Annie Sanders. Annie's writing partner is Meg Sanders. Their novels are published by Orion and include: *Goodbye, Jimmy Choo*; *Warnings of Gales*; *The Xmas Factor*; *Busy Woman Seeks Wife*; *The Gap Year for Grown ups*; *Getting Mad, Getting Even*.

You'll know you've found your voice when . . .

- You start writing something different.
- You can't stop writing this different type of novel.
- It feels as though you've found your soulmate (on paper).
- It feels natural.
- Other people say 'Wow!'

`EXERCISE`

A three-step exercise to help you find your voice

Sit down and write anything that comes into your head for five minutes. Do the same at lunch time. And in the evening.

Now repeat the exercise three times the following day but in a different setting, such as a library or your office.

Re-read all your pieces. Does the style seem different? If so, did you find yourself writing more comfortably with one than the other? ▪

`EXERCISE`

A two-step exercise to help you find your voice

Try writing the first chapter of a different type of novel. If you have always been trying to write romantic fiction, have a go at a thriller. If you have been writing sci-fi, try a historical instead. Don't be afraid to cross your comfort boundaries by tackling a 'genre' that seems alien at first.

Ask a writing friend whom you admire to read your chapter. I don't always encourage writers to show their work to others. But sometimes it can help – and I think that this is one example. Someone else will be able to say if your voice is different and whether it works ▪

TIP

Read other genres to see if it helps you to discover one that feels natural to you.

A one-step exercise to help you find your voice

Do you usually write in the third person? (eg telling the story from the point of view of a character whom you give a name to.)

If so, try writing in the first person.

Here is an opening sentence to get you going.

Julia knew she was going to marry George when he turned down her application for a mortgage.

Now put it into the first person.

I knew I was going to marry George when he turned down my application for a mortgage.

I don't know about you but I'm much more inspired by the sentence in the first person. It seems to have more of a sparkle and makes us wonder if the heroine only married George in order to get the house she wasn't able to get in the first place.

In other words, it seems to have more of a voice because it stands out.

You can extend this exercise with another step: give the narrator a voice so that he or she stands out as an extra character. This is known as creating the 'omniscient' narrator.

Here is an example:

Some people might think Julia was merely calculating when she set her cap at George. Others – perhaps the more gullible – insisted that the fact that he turned down her mortgage application had nothing at all to do with the fact that nine months later, he walked her down the aisle and virtually

straight out into the handsome Georgian house which he owned (in full)
bang opposite the church.

The above paragraph also has a voice. Why? Because we are intrigued by
the narrator. Whose side is he or she on? Does he/she really think Julia is
being mercenary? Whatever the answer, we might read on because we're
intrigued ■

SUMMARY

◆ Finding your voice is like trying out different throat pastilles to
  see which ones work for you. Try writing in different styles and
  see which ones feel natural – as though you've discovered a
  long-lost friend.

◆ If you're not sure, take your pieces to a writing group or ask a
  friend whose advice you value. Read them out and see which
  ones go well.

◆ Experiment by writing with a friend. Each one of you could
  write alternate chapters. Or you could take a character each
  and write the dialogue for that person.

◆ Play around with the first and third person.

◆ Try out different genres such as historicals or sci-fi or romantic
  fiction or thrillers.

4

The Killer First Sentence

No – this hasn't suddenly turned into a How To Write Crime book. But you do need to know how to knock 'em dead with that first sentence. The truth of the matter is that at the time of writing, it's not easy to get your book published, let alone find an agent. But you can maximise your chances of being read (at least to the end of the first page) if your sentence insists that the reader has to go on. It has to be powerful. It has to have that voice we've just been talking about. It has to reel the reader in like a fish with bait that's so tempting the fish cannot ignore it.

Let me give you an example. When I was about 15, I picked up a book in Harrow Library where I used to spent most of my weekends, and read the first lines of a novel. The line went like this. '*As soon as they put me in the ambulance, I knew I was dead.*'

That sent terrible shock waves through me. It was both terrifying and exciting at the same time. I wanted to read on but probably because I was still quite young, I put it back. But that sentence has haunted me ever since. And although it's not the kind of book I normally read, I would like to find it now and just see what happened. That's the test of a killer first sentence.

SO HOW DO YOU COME UP WITH ONE OF YOUR OWN?

A killer first sentence has got to – in my opinion – do one or more of the following things. It has to:

- get inside someone's head so well that you are that person and need to know what happens to them

- create tension so you simply have to read on in order to find out what happens next

- perhaps be funny so that you are amused and want to carry on being amused

- have that 'Yes, That's Me!' quality which reaches out to you and makes you identify with the character or the situation or both.

It could have an unusual format or style or anything which makes the words leap out of the page. For example, it might be a text message that initially draws your eye because it's not the normal pattern of words on the first page. However, that text message won't be enough on its own to be a killer first sentence because the content also has to make you sit up. It could also be a voicemail. Or it could be running the words together so there aren't any gaps between words so the reader has to pause to decipher them. I do this in several of my novels to depict a harassed heroine and it's become a trademark. However, you can't do this for large chunks of text or else the reader will get frustrated. It's more of a gimmick to make the first line stand out. You could also write a sentence without any punctuation at all. Or in another language.

It could be the most beautiful use of prose or description which draws you into the setting so you don't want to let it go.

Here's an example of the first paragraph in my novel *The Wedding Party.*

CHAPTER ONE

Becky

'Ohmigodwhereisshe?Stupidstupidsillywomanshouldhavebeenherehalfan hourago. I'mgoingtobelateforwork.It'sabloodynuisance,that'swhatitis.'

After that, there is space between each word. But the point is that it draws the eye to the words and shows that the character is in a panic.

EXERCISE

You knew this was coming! I'd like you to write your own examples of killer first sentences. But where do you start? Have a look through your Ideas book (see Chapter 1), where you've written down all those ideas that have come to you. Pick the one that appeals most to you and then write that first sentence. Read it through. Can you sharpen it? Can you make it more powerful? ▪

Here are some examples of first sentences from some of my students to get you going.

Emily knew she was going to marry Jack from the minute he walked into the Ladies by mistake.

Quite nice but a little wordy. How about

Emily knew she would marry Jack on the Tuesday that he walked into the Ladies – just as she was washing her hands.

The detail makes it more real, doesn't it. And it's certainly an unusual scene which has potential for humour and character development as well as story.

Here are some more examples of first sentences from my classes.

If he does that one more time, she told herself, she'd kill him.

Amelia knew it was her ex-husband, the minute she saw him on Crimewatch.

John used to be a Jane until the operation.

It was when she realised it was Tuesday and not Monday, that she remembered what she should have been doing last Friday.

' *Don't begin with a long description of the weather! Write a gripping first page and make sure that your main character is sympathetic, so that the reader cares about what happens to her/ him.*)

Susie Vereker, author of *Pond Lane and Paris*; *An Old-Fashioned Arrangement*; *Paris Imperfect*; *Tropical Connections*.

CAN YOU LIVE UP TO THE PROMISE OF THAT FIRST SENTENCE?

A killer first sentence is all very well. You've persuaded the agent to sit down and read it. But now you've got to exercise your charms as a writer and make him sit down until the bottom of the first page.

So how do you do that?

For a start, make sure you haven't written yourself into a hole with that first sentence. If, going back to that first sentence I read in the library, you are lying dead in an ambulance, you've set yourself a challenge. You are going to need to describe what it is like being dead. You may have the kind of imagination that will allow you to do that but personally, I write best about what I know. You could get out of it with a second sentence that says something like '*At least, I thought I was dead. But then I realised from the conversation, that my heart was still going*'.

Would that be a cop out? I think it would be more intriguing if the person really was dead and took us into another world, a bit like *The Five People You Meet in Heaven* by Mitch Albom where the narrator is taken back through his past life to look at people he influenced when he was alive.

Here's an example of what we could do with the student's sentence about Jack going into the loo.

Emily knew she was going to marry Jack from the minute he walked into the Ladies by mistake.

'Whoops. Sorry!'

A pair of brown eyes (matching his cord trousers) met hers just as she was drying her hands.

'Thought this was the Gents.'

Another smile. 'They ought to make the signs on the door a bit clearer, don't you think?'

At the time, Emily had thought this was a genuine mistake. It was only later, when she knew Jack better, that she realised the truth. But by then, it was too late.

I rather like the look of this, don't you? It's an interesting situation and we've got the warmth of character to match it, as well as the promise of tension.

EXERCISE

Study the first lines of different novels including genres (types of books) that you don't normally read.

Now repeat the exercise you did in the middle of the chapter but go on to write the next two or three paragraphs. If they won't come or you don't feel they work, try another first sentence ■

> ❛ *The hook at the beginning of a novel is the most important thing of all. You're not just selling to the ordinary reader in the shop or library. You're hooking the editor or publisher. When I was revising my novel, I decided the opening was too tame. So I took a chapter from the middle and made it into a prologue in the opening. It gave it more impact. That section was vital to the middle so I linked the two. It shows that your original beginning can change.* ❜

> Frances Clamp, author of several books and Winner of the Society of Women Writers and Journalists Clemence Dane Cup 2009.

FULL CIRCLE

When you get to the end of your novel (a fantastic achievement, even if it isn't THE one to get published), go back to the beginning. See if you can end the book with a sentence that matches the beginning. This is sometimes known as 'book-ending'. It might be that you repeat the first sentence at the end. Or it could be that you parody it in different ways. For example, in my books, I always have a section at the end that reflects the problems at the beginning and how they are solved. In *Second Time Lucky*, which begins with an advert for a beautiful house converted into apartments, it ends with another For Sale sign.

TIP

Also see the section on beginnings and endings in Chapter 6 on plot.

EXERCISE

Make a list of first lines from books that you've read. Which ones work for you? Try them out on a friend or a writing group for feedback ■

SUMMARY

♦ A first sentence has to reel the reader in like a powerful piece of bait.

♦ It could excite the reader. Make him/her laugh. Astound him with its beauty. But it has – above all – to have a 'voice' that insists the reader goes on.

♦ A powerful first sentence needs to have the potential to go on. In other words, don't write something so unrealistic that you can't follow it up.

❝ *Remember that your first efforts – or even all your efforts – can be as private as you like. You can't practise the trombone without everyone hearing your mistakes but you can write in your bedroom and no one need know how bad those first efforts are. And if your first efforts are bad, it doesn't mean you won't make it. We all have to learn our craft.*

Katie Fforde, author of numerous bestselling novels and chair of the Romantic Novelists Association.

5

It's All in the Plot: Part One

Plotting is such a complex task (and joy!) that I'm going to deal with it in two chapters. However, it will also creep into other chapters in this book so please don't just read this and the next one, and feel that you have covered it.

WHAT'S YOUR PROBLEM?

The most important point to remember in a novel is that a plot will only work if there's a problem. Your character needs to have a problem in order to move the story along – otherwise it will ramble and bore the reader. Your character might not solve the problem until the end of the novel, in which case you need a good problem which can be spun out. Or else he/she might solve it halfway through – and then you'll need another problem to take over, otherwise the story flags. I also believe that the problem has to make the characters, and the reader, ask lots of questions.

With my latest novel *The Wedding Party*, there are four major problems to begin with because the novel is told from the point of view of four characters. Becky's problem is that she is trying to juggle marriage/children and that she isn't happy about her father getting married again. She also has problems with her own marriage, which evolve as the novel progresses. Helen's problem is that her fiancé wants to tie the knot but she is having second thoughts because her ex-husband (Becky's dad) is getting married again. Mel, a vicar, has a big problem; a hit-and-run driver has knocked over her daughter (who remains in a coma until the end) and she can't quite work out if she can forgive him or not. Because those problems might be too heavy, Mel also has to deal with an unexpected crush on a parishioner (the groom, whose wedding she is due to conduct). And Janie has a problem because she is a very bad wedding planner. So she sets up her own business with an elderly neighbour called For Weddings and a Funeral and then has to decide between her ex who is a rat and a new boyfriend who can't speak English.

I'm hoping that you will see there is potential for all these problems; as soon as one is half-solved, there's another waiting to take its place. There's also a mixture of hard-hitting events and humour – an essential. In addition, there are some restful periods in the plot because you can't have a series of hard-hitting events without the reader feel exhausted. That might be fine for some adventure novels but not for the kind of books I write.

What if it sags?

Often you will reach a stage in your novel where you are aware that the story is not as exciting as you had hoped. Maybe you don't know what to write next. Or perhaps the character doesn't know what to do. This is when you need to 'up the ante'. In other words, increase the odds against your character succeeding in his/her fight to solve the problem.

Let me give you an example. Janie reaches the stage where she has met the man of her dreams even though he doesn't speak English. Enter the rat of an ex-boyfriend who promises he has changed.

What should she do? Fate decides for her because her mobile is stolen – with the dream boyfriend's number on it. And when he rings to track her down, her elderly business partner says she's with the ex. This development hopefully adds extra tension.

Here's another one. Geoff, the groom, is about to finally get married at the end of the novel. But then something happens that could jeopardise the marriage going ahead. Can you guess what that might be? I don't want to reveal it just yet...

Here are some ideas that might help you 'up the ante' or increase tension, or simply introduce something else into the plot.

- ◆ A new character.
- ◆ A new setting.
- ◆ Christmas.
- ◆ Getting into trouble with the law.
- ◆ Going on holiday.
- ◆ A letter (email/answerphone).
- ◆ A journey (missed train?).

EXERCISE

I'd like you to add at least six more ideas to the above list.

Now think of your own plot. How can you increase the odds against your heroine? ■

I DON'T BELIEVE IT!

Sometimes, a writer gets so carried away with the plot that he/she writes himself into a trouble spot. In other words, the writer creates a plot that simply isn't believable. For example, a bride doesn't get married because she finally discovers the groom is really a woman. Yes, I know this has happened in real life. But the weird thing about writing fiction is that sometimes real life is stranger than the story. Yet the reader won't always believe it.

If you feel a little voice inside you asking 'Would this really happen?', take notice of it. Don't brush it under the carpet and insist that it would because you've spent ages writing that scene and you don't want to 'waste' it.

You might well need to find a different problem. Or, alternatively, you could make one of your characters question it, saying what the reader is also asking. 'Why didn't the bride know, in today's day and age, that the groom was really a woman?'

Perhaps it's because they had decided not to get intimate beforehand. Or perhaps it's because the sex change operation had been very realistic!

Either way, you need to ensure your problem is one that people will believe or else they might just put down your book.

WHAT IS A SUB-PLOT AND DO I NEED ONE?

A sub-plot is a minor story that runs alongside the main plot. It can provide a different approach to the main story by introducing humour or another story line. A sub-plot can also throw light on the existing story.

For instance, with *Pride and Prejudice*, you could argue that the sub-plot is about Jane and Bingley, because the main thrust of the action is about Elizabeth and Darcy. However, the two are definitely woven up in each other.

If you are writing multi-character viewpoint novels, there isn't any need for a sub-plot although you can still include one if you want. I don't because I feel that there are already four main story lines going on with my multi-character approach and I don't want to complicate things.

THE MECHANICS OF PLOTTING

Before getting down to the nitty gritty, let me ask you a question.

What do you think is most important in a novel? Character or plot? Some people swear by the first; others by the second. My feeling is that it's a mixture of the two. But how does that help you plot your novel? And should you think of the plot first and the characters second – or the other way round?

I have some writer friends who will spend ages working out what kind of characters they want to write about. It might be a mother of five who suddenly finds herself on her own. Or it could be a man whose wife goes missing. They will write several lists, detailing the kind of personality traits that each character has. They might, for example, write down 'fussy' or 'over-helpful' or 'forgetful'. And they will also make notes on what that character looks like in their heads.

All these points are important and are covered in my chapter on characterisation. However, I personally believe that you need to have some kind of idea about the plot first. It need not be very detailed; it could be just an outline. But it should be enough to then make you think about the kind of characters who will live in that plot. Then when you have those people in your mind, they will become real enough to guide you with the plot.

I know this is a bit complicated to take in so I'm going to go into this idea more deeply below.

PLOTTING A BOOK – THE SOPHIE KING WAY!

I must stress that this is how I do it! It's not necessarily the right way and it's certainly not the only way. But when I first started writing novels, I tried other methods (like the A–Z which I describe later in the chapter) and I didn't find they worked for me.

So here goes! I start by getting the germ of an idea for a novel. I might get this idea through reading something in a paper or talking to a friend or seeing something happen. Or it might just jump into my head.

For instance, with *The Wedding Party*, I was aware there is a trend for middle-aged couples to get married again after a divorce. That led me to wonder what it would be like if a couple was getting married and not many of the guests knew the bride. Hopefully you can feel the tension beginning to creep in here! Tension is crucial for a plot. It's what makes a reader turn the pages. So you, as the writer, have to think of ways to make the reader want to know what is going to happen. You have to build in a situation which could go either way. In the case of my novel, this could be a marriage made in heaven – or in hell.

Then I began to think about the characters. It would be too obvious to centre on the bride and the groom because that's what everyone would expect with a book called The Wedding Party. But it might be more interesting to lead the reader down a series of different routes so he/she wasn't sure if the bride was a goodie or a baddy until the end. The only way of doing this would be to watch her development through the eyes of people who were going to the wedding.

So who would be going? Again, it would be too obvious just to make them relatives or friends. But supposing I included the kind of relative whom you wouldn't expect – such as the groom's ex-wife. And also his grown-up daughter. This would create conflict, which is essential in a plot if the daughter wasn't keen on her father getting married again.

But I still didn't feel this was enough. I wanted to create some more surprise by introducing the kind of 'guests' whom we might not have thought about. So how about the vicar who would of course be female to add a bit more controversy. I say this, not because women vicars are the rarity they were a few years ago but because I could make my vicar into a harassed mum with two difficult teenagers. She could also have come into the Church at a relatively late age – having been in advertising before. We're verging on to the chapter on characterisation now but can you see how, at the same time, it's closely linked to plot? By setting my vicar character like this (in fact her name is Mel), I'm allowing opportunities for plot development because we might just be interested in how a vicar combines her calling with two teenagers who tell her to 'foxtrot oscar'.

Then the fourth main character. As you might have guessed by now, my voice is writing from the point of view of four characters. This seems a reasonable number for the reader to concentrate on (for more advice on number of characters, see Chapter 6 on characterisation). The fourth character, I decided, would be the wedding planner. But not just any wedding planner.

She was going to be dyslexic, which meant she had got things wrong before in previous jobs because she had mis-read words and times. I know a few dyslexic people and have found out how hard it can be for them.

Then, when I had the bones of my characters in my head, they began to give me ideas for the plot. A strong vicar with a background in advertising needed to be 'tested'. So I threw in a big incident which meant she began to question her faith and, into the bargain, have romantic feelings for the groom.

Meanwhile, the groom's ex-wife began to wonder if she was doing the right thing in getting married again. And that led to her doing something she hadn't even thought of before the news that her ex-husband was getting married again. I'm not going to tell you what that was or it would spoil the story. But I hope you can see now how plot and character are inextricably linked and that one thing leads to another.

Meanwhile, I began to consider the structure of the plot as a whole by looking at the timespan. It can be very helpful for the reader if there's a ready-made structure such as the days of the week (my first novel was set from Monday to Sunday). So I decided to set *The Wedding Party* in a nine-month span. To make this clear, I headed the first section: *Nine months to go*. The second section (a few chapters after that) was called *Eight months to go*. And so on. The 'gimmick' was that people picking up the book might think it referred to a pregnancy. But in fact it was to do with a countdown to a wedding.

I call this the coat hanger technique. If you can think of a structure that neatly divides itself into segments, it makes it easier to write. That's why family sagas can flow so well: it's because they are divided into years, e.g. 1890–1902.

EXERCISE

Think of some possible plot ideas that have a natural structure, e.g. a love affair between two people who shouldn't be in love, told through a series of letters because this is the only way they can communicate without being found out.

Here are some other possible plot structure ideas:

◆ A weekly evening class (divided into sections that relate to the different weeks).
◆ A diary.
◆ A bus route. Stories about people on the same bus every day ▪

Look at your Ideas book!

By this stage, I had also begun to think of certain things that would fit into the plot, although I wasn't sure exactly where they would go in. I would get these ideas through a chance thought that came into my head during conversation or something on the radio or television or something that caught my eye while working in my job as writer in residence or walking the dog. I would write them down quickly in my Ideas book. Later, when writing my novel, I would leaf through my notebook and remind myself of some of these ideas so I could slot them in.

At this point, I started writing my first chapter. I knew I wanted to start with Becky, the groom's grown-up daughter, because she was quite strong in my head. Part of her was the harassed young journalist I had been – and still was (although without the 'young') until quite recently. I also know of several 'youngish' people whose parents have divorced and married other people.

Make something happen in each chapter!

When I write a chapter, I always have at least one or two big events that happen in it. I do this in order to keep the reader's attention and to stop the pace from flagging. A flagging pace equals a bored reader! In other words, if a book goes on and on without much happening, the reader becomes fed up.

I usually start my novel, as I said in the killer sentence chapter, with the words run together to show a stressed mother. So I did this in the first chapter where Becky is leaving for work but can't go until her laid-back mother's help arrives to look after her children. I also try to begin with humour because it's a good way of roping the reader in – when the children tell the mother's help that Mummy said she was a 'nuisance' because she was late. This is a situation that has certainly happened to me and may have happened to you.

After that, Becky goes to her magazine office and has to cope with her story disappearing on the computer and then her father ringing to say he is getting married. There are also hints that her own marriage isn't great.

When I finish a chapter, I always write down a couple of ideas for my next chapter. That gives me some ideas to work on subconsciously. I never sit down and think about what I'm going to write but if I know which direction I am going in, the ideas tend to come in better. So for the next chapter, I just wrote:

Helen: ex-wife. Reaction when hears her ex-husband is remarrying.

I wanted Helen to have an interesting job that would allow me to bring in colour and smell and nature in contrast with Becky's magazine job. So I made her a gardener. I also opened the second chapter with her hearing about her ex-husband through her daughter. That often happens in divorced families; indeed, I remember having to ring my father to tell him that my mother had died, which was extremely unreal. So in the second chapter, I have Helen's mixed feelings on hearing the news through a phone call, which in turn, sheds more light on Becky's character even though the viewpoint is Helen's. Then Helen finds herself getting into her van and driving back to the family home she once shared with her ex, Geoff, before their divorce.

By now it has been sold – indeed two more owners have lived in it since then. But the new one, Robin, happens to spot her van with LADY GARDENER on the outside and asks if she would be free to maintain his garden because his wife is an invalid and he can't do it himself. For some reason, which she can't explain to herself, she agrees without telling him that the garden was once hers. Think Moses and Miriam here.

I still hadn't sat down and worked out the plot from A–Z. To me, that would destroy the whole exciting stage of writing the novel. I used to do this with earlier books that didn't get published but found it took the spontaneity out of it. However, I accept that some people prefer this method so I will talk about that in the next section. In the meantime, I want to carry on and show how I do it my way.

At this stage, I prefer to write because the story is forming in my head alongside the characters. It might well be that the plot is becoming a little woolly or spread out. But this is something I can address later on. Providing I keep the 'two main events per chapter' rule in my head, the plot should be fast enough. At the same time, I try to ensure there are enough 'rest and relaxation' periods in a chapter. Otherwise there's too much action and the reader is exhausted. We need to alternate the action with some reflective time for the characters and, of course, setting, smells, colour and the normal things that happen to people such as birthdays, going to the gym and having a nice meal.

I also try to make sure that the main problem is partly solved by the middle of the chapter but that another problem then emerges which has to be sorted out and maybe a third problem. For instance, in *The Wedding Party*, Janie the wedding planner loses her job at the beginning. Then she sets up on her own but discovers that her boyfriend has been unfaithful. She kicks him out but can't afford the rent. Enter Marjorie, her elderly neighbour who suggests she finances Janie and they start a 'For Weddings and a Funeral' business, organising the services for both. Problem solved? Only until things start to go wrong and they play the wedding march at a funeral. Then Janie meets her true love, but just as things look as though they're going right, she loses her purse with his number. Her cheating ex turns up and she falls for him again ... I won't go on but you can see that with just Janie alone, one problem is solved only to lead to another.

How do I think of all these different problems? Sometimes they just come to me and at other times, I ask myself the question 'What if?' What if things happened a different way? I also find that if my characters are strong enough, they will knock on the door of my head and demand that I do something I hadn't thought of. For instance, there's a twist three-quarters of the way through when Helen's dog does something that changes the plot dramatically. I won't tell you what, because it will change the story but the idea came from a combination of Helen's character and my own dog.

At the end of my novel, I print it all out and read it through. I buy another hard-backed exercise book and divide it into sections under the characters. Under the character headings, I write down the plot outlines, showing what happens to each. Then I make sure that all the ends are tied up by the end. Sometimes, I re-jig bits of the plot so they work. And sometimes this means re-writing the beginning or other parts of it. Then I print out again and go through it to check for more loose ends. For example, I might have said the heroine was going to give birth in five months but it's more like eleven by the time we get there! I also take a red pen and strike out all those bits which are repetitive or where the pace flags. If *you* feel something is a bit boring, the reader certainly will. I'm giving more advice on this later on under Revision (see Chapter 16).

There's no such thing as writers' block. Just write something. It can be a load of rubbish. If you're going to write the best sentence ever, you'll sit there for months. But if you write something, you might look back and realise it isn't such rubbish after all. You can do things with it.

Always read your work out loud. It doesn't have to be so everyone can hear it. In your head is fine. You'll learn then from the rhythm, what works and where you need to put a comma or full stop.

I think the plot is more important than the characters. Look at different situations and ask yourself what would happen if something had happened differently.

Unless you're a genius, the best way to get an original idea is to drink a bottle of single malt scotch. I had to give up drinking about six years ago because I got too many ideas and was getting through much scotch.

You need to write about what you know. When it comes to character, most people only know themselves. So use yourself in lots of different characters. Ask yourself what qualities you have as a writer that are most valuable as a person. Then use it. All you have to do to flesh out a character is to get them to think of something.

Colin Dexter, author of *The Inspector Morse* series.

6

It's All in the Plot: Part Two

The previous chapter dealt with my own method of plotting: a mixture of making notes in advance and also writing whatever comes into my head (largely because the characters are hopefully strong enough to 'tell' me what they want me to do with them). Or, to put it another way, something comes into my head when I am describing them that tells me what I should do with their lives.

However, this method doesn't work for everyone. So below, I've explained some other plotting methods which might appeal to you.

THE A–Z METHOD

Some of my students – particularly the ones who have very logical jobs or who haven't written much creatively before – find this method very reassuring. It works like this. The writer has an idea and also, hopefully, has got some characters in mind. He or she then sits down and writes out a plot from beginning to end. It might be a few notes. Or it could be several pages per chapter.

Then the writer goes back to the beginning and elaborates on those notes or chapter pages. The plus side is that they feel they have done a lot of the work already so the 'task' of writing a novel is not so daunting. When they sit down at a desk, they have a 'blueprint' to steer them. So even if they've had a break of a few days or weeks or even longer, they can remind themselves with their 'literary knitting pattern' of what happens next.

However, in my view, the 'strength' of this approach is also its weakness. Why? Because the downside is that this method forces you to work out what is going to happen in a novel BEFORE the characters have had a chance to get going. In other words, before you really get to know them as people. It's a bit like promising to stay with someone for the rest of their life even though you only have a slight acquaintance. And yes – it can work! Both in fiction and in real life. You probably have at least one friend who decided to get married after one or two dates and you're about to tell me they've just celebrated their Golden Wedding. But it's rare. Why? Because we need to know someone's in's and out's, so to speak, before we can really set off on a long journey with them. And that's the same with your novel.

So if your plot outline tells you that you need to send your heroine Betty to the country to become a nanny to a widower's three difficult children, that's fine. But when writing the novel and you grow to know Betty, you might find that, at the last minute, her application for that job in Dubai comes up and she decides to go there instead.

And what's wrong with that? You'll plump for Dubai instead. But will you? The funny thing about writing a plot outline is that you can spend quite a long time on it. So if that little voice inside you suggests that you change it, you might well hear a louder voice saying 'Rubbish! I've written my plot outline and I'm not going to waste all that time I spent creating it, so the country it is!'

And that's a shame. Because a strong character will, as you'll see in Chapter 7 on Characterisation, direct you. He or she will tell you which way to go in a story. It might not happen when you are actually writing it. But it *will* at some point when you're probably doing something else like washing up or feeding the cat. You'll have one of those Eureka moments in the supermarket when you're buying Dutch cheese and realise that what Betty needs to do is to open up a deli in Gloucestershire instead!

Compromise A–Z

There's usually a happy compromise in life and here's one for that A–Z. It involves being both practical and imaginative. You write a brief plot outline, e.g. Betty's boyfriend dumps her and she loses her flat at the same time. So she chucks in her job and decides on a complete career change.

You will also have started to think about Betty's character (see Chapter 7) and, at the same time, you will start to make notes about the plot in your notebook. These will be ideas that come to you as you go around your day-to-day business. And then you start writing. If you come to something in your plot outline which is quite specific but, by then, you feel your character wouldn't act in such a way, you need to be prepared to alter the plot from the blueprint you have created for yourself. So if, in your plot outline, you make Betty fall in love with the widower but then feel that is too predictable when you get there, allow yourself to consider an alternative. Perhaps she falls in love with his older son instead who is an adult but still younger than she is.

One advantage, it has to be said, for the compromise A–Z plan, is that it will be helpful for you when you write the synopsis. I've dedicated a special chapter to this (Chapter 17) because synopses are not easy to write. This is because you have to tell the whole story from beginning to end which is impossible if you haven't actually written it. But if you have a rough plot outline from your A–Z, it's easier!

THROW AND SCATTER METHOD

This is a rather fun method of plotting, which can be used to create an entire plot or stage within the whole plot to move it on. (I call these 'plot-pushers'.) It works like this. You write an A–Z for a plot and then cut up the different events so you have a series of cards with action scenes on them. It might be four cards that read in turn: 'Douglas meets the woman next door' and 'Douglas' wife buys a puppy because she feels rejected' and 'Susan, their daughter, goes on a blind date' and 'Tom, their son, has a car accident but survives with a broken leg'. You might see this initially as a chronological series of events. But then try throwing them all in the air and see what they come down as. You might have a plot that starts with the broken leg and then goes on to the woman next door and then the date and then the puppy. This might sound like a bit of a silly example but the sillier the better, at first! It makes it stick in your mind.

Another alternative is to write random sentences down on separate cards. Try picking these sentences from a newspaper or magazine or odd conversations you hear. Then throw them in the air and see what order they come down with. Does it suggest a plot? Here's a mixture of sentences from my local paper plus a conversation I had with my decorator this morning. 'Man finds old coin in back garden.' 'Sally raises £10,000 in charity dive'. 'Husband delivers baby daughter in car park. 'What's this stain on the carpet?' Now throw these cards in the air and see if they make you think of a plot!

FEELING BOARD?

No, I haven't spelt 'board' wrong. It's a pun to make you aware
of another plotting technique. This one appeals to people with a
visual mind. It's quite simple. You need either a whiteboard in
front of your desk or a corkboard. If it's the first, you write down
ideas for your plot and because they're on a whiteboard, you can
wipe them off when you change your mind and add more ideas.

The plus with this idea is that every time you sit down and look at
it, you might feel inspired to change things or get writing. The
minus is that someone else might accidentally wipe this off. This
happened to me when one of my children decided he needed to
draw a picture himself. (I also had a terrible experience when
another of my sons turned off the trip switch and I lost a chapter
of my novel in the days when computers didn't have automatic
back ups...)

The corkboard is more reliable because it's harder to erase.
Instead, you pin your ideas on to cards – the different coloured
index cards in newsagents are great for this. Again, they act as a
reminder for your novel so you're always in the zone; in other
words, you remember what the story line is. And they can also
be moved around to make different sequences of events. Try it
and see!

TREE DIAGRAM

This is a cracking way of checking that you have enough going on
in your plot. You can also use it to check you have enough going

on in each chapter. Basically, it's a form of mind mapping. And it works like this:

Draw a long vertical line down the middle of a blank A4 piece of paper. Down the side, write down one line which sums up your novel. For example, if I was to do this for *The Wedding Party*, I would write: This is the story of four women involved in a wedding which is due to take place in nine months' time.

Then, draw a sloping line going upwards, like a branch, starting at the bottom of your vertical line and to the right of it. On that line, you sum up that chapter. So mine would be: Becky is upset to find out that her father is getting married again. That is the main piece of action in Chapter 1. But there are other things going on too which aren't quite so dramatic. I would put these underneath the line in brackets, e.g. (Becky finds it difficult to cope with her children and finds it a relief to go into the office. Problem with losing work on computer.)

Then I would draw another line above that which depicts Chapter 2. In that, I would write: Helen finds out that her ex-husband is getting married. She drives to old home and is hired as a gardener by the new owner who doesn't know she used to live there years ago. Then, in brackets, I would put (Helen makes arrangements to see David, her fiancé that evening).

I would carry on up the right-hand side of the tree and then down the other, using each 'branch' or line to sum up the chapter. Why? The aim is to make sure that you have enough going on in each branch. If you find that the so-called 'action events' mainly consist of a character talking to herself about a difficult situation without anything actually HAPPENING, your pace will probably be too slow. And a slow pace = boredom for the reader. Well, usually, anyway.

On the other hand, if each branch is packed with so many action events that you run out of room to cram everything on that branch, you might well have too much going on!

A good book is like a good walk. Or an interesting journey. You need to smell new scenes; taste different experiences; be entertained. But at the same time, you also need time to relax or 'chillax' as my kids call it. If you don't, your reader is going to be exhausted. And that means he/she may not appreciate the impact of the powerful scenes because there are so many of them.

A tree diagram will help you work out if you've got the right balance, especially if you're a visual kind of person who needs to picture things in front of you.

You can also include the sub-plot in your tree diagram. The best way to do this is to write it along the same branch but in a different coloured pen to make it stand out.

EXAMPLE

On page 76 is an example of the tree diagram using Little Red Riding Hood, as that is a story most of you will know.

The writing along the long vertical line in the middle, should sum up the story. (Little girl visits grandmother and is saved from wolf by woodcutter.) Then there is a series of diagonal lines, starting from the bottom right. Each one represents a change in action or what I call a gear change. They are labelled as follows:

First bottom line: Mother tells her daughter Red Riding Hood to visit grandmother. **Q**. ('Q' stands for quiet piece of action.)

Second line: Red Riding Hood meets wolf and they have a chat. **A**. This stands for 'action'.)

Third line: Wolf runs on and eats grandmother. **A**.

Fourth line: Red Riding Hood arrives and asks grandmother why she has such a big nose and ears, etc. **Q**.

Fifth line: Wolf tries to gobble Red Riding Hood up. **A**.

Sixth line: Woodcutter rushes in and saves Red Riding Hood as well as chopping open the wolf and releasing grandmother. **A**.

Seventh line: Mother, grandmother and Red Riding Hood are reunited and thank woodcutter. **Q**.

You can see from the resulting tree that there is a good display of branches and that there is also a mixture of Q and A, representing a nice balance of action events and quieter periods.

Tying up loose ends in your plot

Another advantage of the tree diagram is that it can help you tie up loose ends in your plot. If you've written on branch one that your heroine is planning a surprise birthday for the hero, you need to check that the birthday appears somewhere on the tree. It sounds simple, doesn't it, but believe me, it's very easy for a promised birthday to get lost along the way because you've thought of more interesting things to happen in the plot.

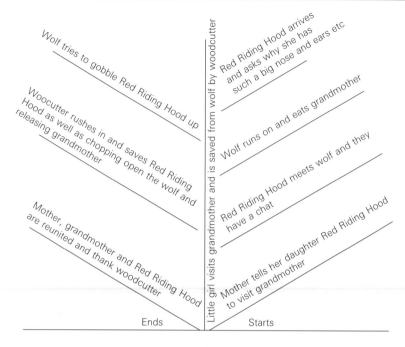

Tree diagram

Another useful way of checking you haven't left something out, is to buy yourself another hard-backed A4 book (apart from your Ideas book). Divide the first page into quarters (I'm assuming here that you don't have more than four main characters) and, in each quarter, write essential information about your character, e.g. name; who married to; children; job; age, etc.

If you have minor characters too, do the same for them on another page in different coloured ink.

As you develop your characters, expand those quarter pages into sections with the main character's head at the beginning. You could, if you like, add a picture of those characters if you've found someone similar in a magazine (more details on this in Chapter 7 on characterisation).

I suggest you do this while you're writing your novel, but when you get to the end of it (yes you will!), go through your manuscript and check you've included all the main events that happen to the character as well as extra details, e.g. Amanda gets engaged.

If you are writing multi-viewpoint novels like mine, where you follow the lives of four main characters, it's worth doing a double check. This involves taking each character and looking just at their story in one thread. In other words, instead of going through the book chapter by chapter, just look for that character's name (you can use the word search to help) and write down what happens to that person as though they were the main character in the novel and it was just about them. Then do the same with the others.

When to use the tree diagram

I personally use it to check that enough is going on, once I have written the whole novel. It might help me spot 'gaps' in my novel where there isn't enough action OR where I have promised that a character will do something such as have a 40th birthday and then realise, from the tree, that I have forgotten to put it in.

However, the tree diagram can also be useful for writers who are committed to the A–Z approach of planning a novel in stages from start to finish before they actually start to write it.

Whichever one you choose, do experiment with tree diagrams. They are really very useful!

PLOTTING YOUR BEGINNINGS AND ENDINGS

We've already talked about killer first sentences (although you might like to read that chapter again). But when you've finished your novel and you go back over it again (see Chapter 16 on Revision), you may find that your opening isn't as relevant any more. It might have changed because you have got into the book more as you've gone on (a good sign) and changed the characters or their motives or their personalities. You might also have changed the plot. In fact, I hope you have because it shows you are adaptable and that the characters are big enough to make you do things and believe in them.

This could mean making the third paragraph into the first paragraph. Or even the second chapter into the first (because it's more interesting and you've got into it) and scrapping the first (although using some of the information).

So don't heave a great sigh of despair and think 'I've got to change the beginning and it's a waste of all my work'. It isn't a waste. It shows you are on the right track.

Endings are a little different. You may well have read a book which seems rushed at the end. I certainly have. Sometimes it's because the author has been told to hurry up by the publisher because the book is late. Sometimes it's because the author is bored with his or her own story. And sometimes it's because the author doesn't know what to do at the end. This can often lead to the most unbelievable situations which cause the reader to lose faith with the author. I personally find this very distressing because it's a breaking of trust. You should not, as the writer, lead your reader down the literary path for 100,000 words plus and then make them feel cheated at the end.

The following is a 'quote' from one of my students in my classes:

I read a book which looked as though it was a true story about a woman's life. When I got to the end, I found it was actually fiction. Then I realised that the front cover actually said it was a work of fiction but in small print. I felt very cheated: if I'd known it was fiction from the beginning, I would have engaged differently with the heroine. But because I thought she was real, I rooted for her in a different way only to find she was a figment of the author's imagination.

DOES AN ENDING NEED TO BE HAPPY?

Not necessarily. Life isn't like that, is it? But it does rather depend on the type of book you are writing. It suits some books to have a hero or heroine who dies or ends up without Mr or Mrs Right. Personally, with my own books, I need my heroine to come out on top and to have conquered most of her problems. But it might be that she has conquered them in a way the reader didn't expect (or the heroine), which in turn, makes the character more of a real person.

And it's perfectly feasible – as well as realistic – for other characters to have an unhappy ending.

An editor once told me that what should be avoided, in most novels, is the ending where you don't know what happens. Again, this can leave the reader feeling cheated. They've invested time and energy in this story (it takes perseverance to get to the end) and they still don't know what happens.

RESEARCH

I've included this section in the plotting chapters because many readers don't know whether to do it at the beginning or the end. My feeling is that it's best to have a certain amount of knowledge before you start and then, after you've got into it (perhaps after a few chapters), to do a bit of research so you know you are going in the right direction. For example, if you were writing about a heroine in an advertising agency, it would be a good idea to know a bit about that world. Perhaps you used to work in it or maybe you know someone who does. So you start your novel but then you want to pitch your heroine into a crisis. It's at this point you need to do some more research so you can find out what kind of crisis. I'd suggest ringing up an ad agency and asking if you can spend the day in the office. Make it clear you're not going to use real names but that you need to soak up the atmosphere. I personally feel this is better than just speaking to someone on the phone about their job. You need to hear and smell and taste the office (what awful coffee!) to make your book real.

Then sandwich your research with your writing: a bit of plot and then research; character development and then research. It will give it an extra burst of energy.

HOW TO PLOT FLASHBACKS

A flashback is where the story darts back in time to cover an important scene or piece of information. In my view, a flashback should be short – otherwise it takes the reader out of the comfort zone you have created and plonks them in a different environment. Then you get them to go back after several pages and you no longer feel you are there with them. Supposing, for example, you write half a chapter about a woman working in

London. A chance meeting with a Frenchman in a bar reminds her of her time in France and she then spends three pages thinking or remembering what happened to her then. After that, the chapter reverts back to that London bar. Your reader will be now be feeling slightly travel sick!

Far better, in my opinion, to either keep the flashback short (say, about three paragraphs) or to distinguish it from the bits before and after either with a row of stars (showing the reader there is going to be a break in time or scene) or even a new chapter.

EXERCISE

So you're stuck! Or bored! Well, if YOU'RE bored, the chances are that your reader will be too. So we need to think of ways to bring the plot on or pep up your characters. I've outlined some ideas below but I'd like you to pick at least three and elaborate. For example, in the 'Crisis' below, consider what kind of crisis you could give a character. Might it be an unexpected pregnancy? Or losing the keys to a neighbour's house when you've promised to feed her cat when she's away? And how would this crisis affect the plot?

- ◆ Crisis.
- ◆ A change – which alters the situation.
- ◆ Birthdays/Christmas/anniversaries. Forgotten. Remembered.
- ◆ Communication or lack of. Letters. Missing emails. Phone calls.
- ◆ Character behaving differently, e.g. drunk.
- ◆ Illness.
- ◆ New characters.
- ◆ Pet problems.
- ◆ House problems, e.g. moving/extension, etc.

◆ Accident.

◆ New places.

◆ Financial problems.

With any luck, you'll have some more ideas now – and you might see your novel in a different light ■

SUMMARY

Wow! There's quite a lot to take in here, isn't there? So instead of my usual summary, I'd like you to go back and read this chapter and the previous one, all over again! Then try the following exercise:

Write an outline of your current novel or one you've written before or one which you have in your head or a book that you are reading and that has been written by someone else. Do a tree diagram (use a different book if you've already done one). Make a list of the 'up the antes' you can do to your heroes or heroines. Think about your beginning and ending in the light of this chapter.

❛ *Pick a book that you've enjoyed recently and a book that you haven't. Write an outline of the plot for each one of them. Is enough happening in the plot? Are there loose ends that the author has failed to tie up? Has he or she made promises with the characters or plot that aren't fulfilled? This might help you to understand what you need to put in the plot in order to get noticed. My view is that not enough would-be authors bother to do this and this is why their books don't get picked up.* ❜

Agent.

7

Who Are You? How to Create Convincing Characters

Do you have a friend who is, let's put it bluntly, boring? Bland without much to them? Nothing that makes them particularly interesting? Maybe you even dread having to talk to him or socialise with her because she's very dull.

If that sounds hard, it's not meant to be. Most of us have a friend like that and if we're nice people – which I hope we are – we carry on being friends with them perhaps because we've known them a long time and it seems wrong to break the ties of friendship. Or maybe they're relatives whom we need to see. But the point is that if we didn't have these bonds, we might not have much to do with them.

Now translate that person into a fictional hero or heroine. Would we be particularly interested in their lives? If they just talked about the weather or their children or what was on television last night, would we be riveted and desperate to turn the next page?

Probably not.

A dull character like this might well work as a minor character, probably because they would be a figure of fun. But I wouldn't recommend Mr or Mrs Boring as the main person in your story because you're not likely to reel your character in.

So how do we create convincing characters?

This is what I feel, we all need to do:

- Give them a problem that will last for the whole novel.

- Use this problem to send them on a journey, either emotional or physical or both, so they change (hopefully for the better) by the end.

- Make them different from each other so there's a clear distinction and the reader doesn't get muddled.

- Ensure the reader likes the hero or heroine, even though they may not (should not, in fact) be perfect.

- Limit the number of main characters so the reader doesn't feel too confused – you can only identify with so many.

- Be careful how you name them.

- Include their 'satellite possessions': in other words, things and people that go with them to create this person, e.g. house, children, car, job, etc.

- Make them believable.

- Remember to give them seasonal events like birthdays, holidays, Christmas, etc.

- Make the most of a villain!

Let's start with the first:

WHAT'S THEIR PROBLEM?

We've already said that if a plot doesn't have a problem, there isn't much of a story. And it's the same for your characters. Think about yourself. Write down four or five big problems that you've had to cope with in life so far.

If you could do more, you've probably got more than enough material for a novel. And if you don't think you've had any problems, you possibly haven't got out of the house enough!

The plus side about having lots of problems is that you've got this experience to write about, although you obviously need to veil the facts. If someone says to me that they can't think of anything big that's happened to them, I question whether they can in fact be a writer. Personally, I feel you write better if you have suffered a bit.

EXERCISE

You've already written down four or five problems that you've had in life. Now write down how you've coped with them.

If you prefer, write down an outline of a problem that someone you know quite well has had to deal with ▨

How can we use this?

Let's take some of the characters and their problems from my fourth novel *The Supper Club*. Chrissie is a new mum who is worried about something happening to her baby. It's something that many new mothers go through. What if that bump on their head is serious? Can they catch something from the child at playgroup who has a bad cold?

The problem for Chrissie is that she actually becomes almost paranoid about it – especially when someone accuses her of having hurt her own child because he's covered in bruises. When this problem is sorted out, Chrissie then has another problem. An ex-boyfriend turns up at her supper club (held in different friends' houses) and threatens to reveal a secret from the past.

If Chrissie had just had the first problem (fussy mother bordering on paranoia), it probably wouldn't be enough. It's important to have a wedge of problems that our characters need to work their way through. I won't tell you what happens at the end but I will say that Chrissie is definitely pleased that she made that emotional journey.

I'm going to take another problem character now: Lucy, the heroine in *The Supper Club* is a youngish widow about to get married again. Her first problem is that her children don't like this idea. Secondly, her mother-in-law (mother of the dead husband) moves in with them. And then Lucy has to cope with a difficult teenage son who runs away from home. All these problems are solved but they overlap and keep the reader on his or her toes. (At least, that's what my loyal readers have told me.) But if she'd just had one problem, that wouldn't have been enough to have kept us going through the book. And, just as important, they tell us about Lucy as a person in the way she handles them. She's basically a kind, honest person who is having to cope with the guilt of her husband's death (she holds herself partly responsible). She also wants the best for her children. And she doesn't want to upset her mother-in-law. When her son goes missing, she is frantic – and sets out to rescue him. She sounds like she'd be an interesting person to sit next to. And that's what we're aiming for. If you don't want to sit next to your hero or heroine, we can't expect our readers to.

EXERCISE

Have a think about the list of problems you've made. Would any of them work for the novel you are thinking about or would like to write or indeed are writing at the moment? Could they be used as 'plot pushers' to move the scene along? What would they add to a character? Would they make the character more real?

Do we still like the character, despite the problems we've given them?

It's important that we do! If we don't like them, we won't want them to overcome the obstacles we've created in their journey. So be careful what you wish for, with your character! If their problem is that they're on the run from someone they've murdered, you might not feel very sympathetic towards them and you won't want them to win. But if they're on the run from someone they murdered in self-defence, that could be another story.

If their problem is, like Bridget Jones, that she's overweight and smokes too much and cannot find a man, we forgive her. In fact, we might applaud her if we feel the same. But if she's a shoplifter, we might not be on her side.

Introduce your heroine as soon as possible – preferably on page 1. An editor once told me that readers are like lemmings. They feel they need to bond with the first character that appears on the page. So if your heroine doesn't appear until page 3, their interest might already be with a minor character on page 1 who isn't very significant in the novel. This in turn can cause them to lose interest or get confused about who is important and who isn't.

WHO'S WHO?

Have you ever read a novel where you confuse the characters? Where you're not sure if Pippa is the one who has left her husband or if that's Caroline? That might be because you haven't made a big enough distinction between the characters. I'm not just talking about how you've described them. It's easy to make the characters look different in terms of physical description. But we need to do it in other ways too. For instance, in the way they speak. If Caroline is a worrier, this will be reflected in her conversation. She might say 'I'm so worried that . . .' at the beginning of each sentence. So when a character starts talking like that or wringing her hands or constantly checking she's shut the front door, the reader will probably think it's Caroline before you even have the 'said Caroline'.

There are lots of other ways too to make your character stand out. What kind of home do they live in and is it immaculately neat or untidy? How many children do they have ? If they have offspring, are they always being interrupted by them or running around after them? If they would desperately like children but haven't had any success so far, are they always buying pregnancy testing kits or waiting for an IVF appointment? What kind of car do they drive? Is it tidy or do they litter it with empty crisp packets and old cartons? What is their job? Does this affect the way they think and behave? In *The Supper Club*, Lucy's sister is an events organiser. When we meet her, she's always doing something related to work and that makes her the kind of character she is.

ARE THEY BELIEVABLE?

We've all met some strange people in life. And if they weren't standing in front of us in flesh and blood, we might think they were made up. But in fiction, you have a more complex challenge. You need to create characters that will stand out but who are also possible human beings. So yes, real people do go back to check the front door all the time. But would they stalk their neighbours without reason to do so? Would they pretend they had been fired when they hadn't, in order to have some 'free time'? It's just possible but, in order to convince the reader, you need to build up the character so they are the kind of person who might just do this. And if so, would we like them considering they are deceptive, or is there a reason for this behaviour that we can sympathise with?

Using magazines and television

One way to make your characters ring true is to cut out pictures from magazines and newspapers that sum up the picture you have in your head for your character. A lot of my students do this and then they stick it in their Ideas book. That redhead with the high cheekbones might look exactly like the person you were thinking of when you were writing about the heroine's sister. And the man with the receding hairline who actually looks very attractive is perfect for her. The great thing about this is that you might not have realised your man had a receding hairline until you saw it in the picture. But now you can put that on paper and it will look real.

TIP

Sit down and watch breakfast television – especially the bit where the presenters interview guests. Write down what the guest looks like; what his mannerisms are like; how he smiles; what he does with his hands. Here is an example I did myself the other day:

Patting air

Crinkly smile with lines on either side

Cord jacket with jeans

Talks as though presenter is the only person in the world who counts.

Now if you made your character do exactly the same, he would be real!

EXERCISE

Sit on a tube or a bus or in a coffee shop and write down your description of people you see around you. What do you think they do? Where are they going? What have they just been doing? Why has he got a scar on his face? Be careful you're not observed or you might get into trouble ■

Too real?

Be very careful about basing your character on a real person, or you could find yourself in legal hot water. Sometimes writers do this without realising. So go over your characters carefully and make sure you change their names so they are completely different and possibly their sex and location too.

EXERCISE

Still stuck on making your characters work? Not sure what job to give them or what they are like as people? Try this.

Place four empty jam jars or mugs in front of you.

Write out a list of ten names – five should be male and five female. The Births, Marriages and Deaths column in the local and national papers are good inspirations, as are baby name books. Cut each name out and put all ten bits of paper into one of the jam jars or mugs.

Write out a list of five characteristics that you like in someone and five that you don't, e.g. kind/friendly, etc. or jealous/mean, etc. Again, cut each characteristic out and put all ten bits in the jam jar/mug.

Write out a list of ten jobs. Try to include unusual ones too, such as wine tasting. Put the ten pieces in the mug.

Write out ten problems that you or someone else has had. These could be small, such as getting a parking ticket or big such as having an affair. Put all ten bits in the jar/mug.

Now take one piece of paper out of a mug and see what you come out with. Here is an example from one of my students:

Gloria, a trainee train driver, has bad time-keeping and is about to start a new job that she knows nothing about.

Well, it certainly gets you thinking, doesn't it? I'm not suggesting you go off and write a novel about Gloria with all the details in the paragraph idea. But it might give you some ideas. Starting a job that your heroine knows nothing about could lead to all kinds of plot-pushers and story development. And that's exactly what we want to keep the reader on his/ her toes ▪

MY FAMILY AND OTHER ANIMALS

Has your character got any relatives? It's amazing how writers completely forget that many of us do – even though it's not always fashionable to remember it! Use your hero or heroine's family wisely. Turn them upside down so they don't do what you expect. A mother doesn't always have to be fussy. Perhaps she's rather laid back and bohemian so it's the children who are fussy instead. A dad doesn't have to work long hours. He might decide to go on a gap year, leaving everyone else at home.

Ask yourself what effect this would have on your main characters. Would it make them feel upset or happy or question their own lives?

I intentionally have a mixture of ages in my novels, ranging from children (these could be babies or teenagers) through to grannies. My grandmother lived with us until I was 12 so I have always got on well with older people and have several friends who are a generation older than me. But I include the different ages for more commercial reasons. I feel they rub off on each other and make the characters do things that they might not otherwise do. And I also feel that they help to make the book appeal to a wider age range.

Animals are another useful way of making your character stand out. They can bring out the warmth in a person – and they can bring out the dark side. A character might seem nice but if he secretly kicks his host's dog under the table because he's after his food, maybe he's a villain after all.

Dogs and other animals can also move the plot along. (I always have a dog in my books because I've had two, myself.) In my second novel *The Supper Club*, the single mother of three moves into a small apartment with her children and their dog. The dog annoys some of the neighbours and leads the way to a plot-pusher which changes the whole story...

One word of caution here – do make sure you know your animal before you write about him or her. Unless you own a cat or dog, it's difficult to get an insight into their characters and their effect on others.

MAKE THE MOST OF YOUR BADDY

The baddy can be great at making your plot move along – and in revealing characteristics about your other characters. Where would we be without Cruella de Ville?

But I think the most interesting baddies are those which don't seem obvious from the beginning. For instance, a character who seems nice but then, as the story progresses, reveals his or her true colours.

This can work the other way too. Someone might seem horrible but then, as the story goes on, you find that actually, they're all right. Think Darcy here from *Pride and Prejudice*.

EXERCISE

Think of someone you know who either seemed nice to begin with and then was shown to be untrustworthy. Or someone who seemed nasty but then proved to be a nice person. If it's the latter, you need to give a reason for this apparent change in temperament. Were they stand-offish because they are actually very shy?

Now think about how you would use these people (or a variation of them) in a novel

MINOR CHARACTERS

We've already said that it's best to limit your main characters to about four. But you can also have the same number or so for minor characters. I wouldn't suggest having more than that because it can confuse the reader but that's a personal opinion.

Minor characters can be great in creating dilemmas for main characters and also showing us something about them. For example, in *The Wedding Party*, there is an archdeacon who interviews Mel the vicar for her job. He seems to disapprove of Mel's large earrings and black boots, but then, as the book goes on, he reveals more about himself and we begin to like him.

Sometimes, in my novels, I include a major character from a previous novel and use them fleetingly as a minor character in the next novel. It's a way of showing the reader what that character has been doing since the last one! And it helps me keep in touch with them. If you really love your characters, you'll be sad when the novel ends and you say goodbye to them...

FIRST DATE RULE

We need to know a lot about our characters, don't we? But the danger is in telling the reader too much too soon. That's when we come on to my first date rule. Don't give out too much on the first date! Don't tell someone everything about you at the beginning or they could be bored, not to mention overwhelmed. It's the same in fiction. You need to spin out their story so we learn bits as the novel goes on.

CHOOSING A NAME

This is crucial. Names mean so much to us, don't they? And

without realising it, your choice of name could make the agent or publisher keener to pick it up – or put it down. If your heroine is called Stephanie, I wouldn't be very keen on that because I used to know a Stephanie and she wasn't very pleasant.

How unfair is that? You, as the writer, don't know that someone dislikes that name. So how can you choose one that everyone will like? The truth is that you can't. But you can raise the odds by choosing a name for your hero or heroine that is friendly. Names which end in 'y' are often good for this.

Also ensure the name isn't too narrow. For example, Arabella suggests a certain type of woman. That's fine if that's the kind of woman you want to show but some readers might be put off, assuming it's a 'posh' book.

Also make sure that your characters' names start with different letters of the alphabet, otherwise it can be confusing. This works from a visual point of view too. So if you have a hero called Geoff, it might not work if you also have a heroine called Gillian. Yes, of course the reader knows they are different because they're different sexes. But because they both begin with 'G', the mind doesn't always recognise it and has to think twice.

HAVE YOU MISSED THEIR BIRTHDAY?

Characters are entitled to birthdays too. And don't forget anniversaries, Christmas and summer holidays. It does two things. It makes it more realistic for the reader because your characters are living in the real world. And it also provides more opportunities to expand the plot. If a character's husband or child forgets his or her birthday, they might justifiably be upset. It might encourage them to do something that's out of character such as taking themselves off for the day or a week or even for ever. And supposing the hero is given a present by his mistress that's exactly the same one that his wife gives him. Is it coincidence or could the wife and mistress have got together and decided to play a joke on him? You can see how this can really be milked!

It's the same for Christmas. This is a fraught time for some of us in the real world. And we can use it to do the same with our make-believe characters. What happens to grown-up children whose parents are divorced? Do they spend Christmas Day with one and then upset the other? If so, what will that do to the absent parent?

Supposing one of your characters has to work at Christmas? Maybe she's a doctor or a nurse or a fireman? How will his or her family spend Christmas Day without them?

Here's a list of other seasonal events to remember when writing your novel:

- Easter.
- Father's Day.
- Mothering Sunday.
- Holidays.
- Anniversaries (weddings; deaths).
- Milestones in life, e.g. ten years since marriage broke up.
- Hallowe'en.
- Valentine's Day.
- Bank holidays.

HOW WELL DO YOU KNOW YOUR CHARACTER?

By now, you might feel you know him or her pretty well. But here's a quiz for you to fill in. Do it for your four main characters and if you don't know the answers, make them up. For instance, if you don't know what kind of toothpaste your hero uses, think of one which will make him stand out. Detail makes a character come to life.

You won't need to use all these details in your character. But it does help to make you feel you really know this person. And that knowledge will come through in your writing so they feel more real to the reader.

QUIZ

What is your character's biggest fear?
What does she want more than anything in the world?
What event has had the biggest impact in his life?
What is his favourite meal?
What kind of books does she like to read (same for films, etc)?
How much does he weigh?
Is she on a diet?
How tidy is her bedroom?
When did she pass her driving test?

Now make up at least ten more questions of your own and see if it helps you to see your character as a more well-rounded person.

TIP

Try to include a wide variety of ages in your characters. This might make the novel more appealing to agents and publishers because it broadens its selling appeal. If you have grannies as well as teenagers and also parents, it stands to reason that three generations might be interested in buying your book rather than just one.

GOING BACK TO THE BEGINNING

When I finish my first draft, I got back to the beginning within a week or so (see Chapter 16 on revision). One of the things I then do is to change things about my characters. When I first start to write a novel, I know a bit about the heroine but not as much as I do by the end. So it makes sense to go back and add those extra details at the beginning. For instance, by the end of the novel, I might have discovered that her mother was sectioned as a teenager – a secret that she kept quiet. So I might drop a couple of hints in some earlier chapters about this – but not so that the reader knows the full story.

This is known as foreshadowing and works equally for both character and plot. Here's another example. I might have a hero who doesn't drive. It isn't until the end of the novel that we discover why – but I could put in a couple of clues at the beginning. For instance, he fobs off questions from others about why he doesn't drive and just says he never got round to it. Then we find out it's because he killed someone by mistake when they ran out in the road in front of him.

EXERCISE

Draw up a list of your characters in the novel you're working on at the moment. Describe them in a letter to someone as though you re introducing them

Let your character tell his or her story. Put him on the stage in front of you.

Rosie Goodwin, author of numerous novels including *A Rose Among Thorns*.

SUMMARY

◆ Know your character inside out – even down to the toothpaste they use and whether they polish the house every day or once a month.

◆ Collect magazine pictures so you know what they look like.

◆ Don't base them on one particular person.

◆ Give them frailties and problems so they are human.

◆ Remember that characters have families and birthdays too!

◆ Name them carefully.

◆ Don't have more than four main characters in a novel (or possibly five).

◆ Make each character work for their living; in other words, ask yourself why you need them in the novel. If you don't need them, you might have to merge them with others.

◆ Remember the 'first date' rule about not giving out too much.

◆ Milk the baddy for all his worth. He can add a lot to a novel.

'*Make sure the reader can picture the character when you introduce him/her. You only need a few lines. Then, every time that character appears again, add a little more detail so a picture slowly emerges.*'

Feresa Chris, agent

8

Viewpoint

When I wrote my very first novel, I was lucky enough to be taken on by an agent. She didn't sell it but I did have some near misses. One editor who turned it down was kind enough to suggest that I came into her office with my agent to give me some advice. I didn't realise at the time how rare that was and I am extremely grateful to her. She said it was because she could see I had potential (again, very kind) but that there was one thing I needed to get straight. And that was 'Viewpoint'.

She took three minutes to explain it and they were three minutes that changed my life. So I'm going to tell you what she told me but I'm also going to add my own 'shoe image' to illustrate it.

Imagine telling a story to someone. You are wearing a pair of blue shoes. Your story is a description of the room in which you are standing and how you are feeling at this very time. You're actually very sad because you have just lost a dear friend. You might express these feelings in dialogue or you might be thinking these feelings.

Now imagine that you are the person that you have been talking to. You are wearing red shoes. You are listening to a woman with blonde hair (goodness, that fringe needs trimming!) telling you about a friend of hers that had died. And although you feel sorry for her (of course you do!), you can't help feeling very excited inside. Why? Because you've just got engaged and you're dying to tell someone although this isn't the time or place to do it because this woman needs comforting.

Both stories have potential to be interesting, don't you think? But they wouldn't look right if they came across like this:

> Marianne didn't mean to tell this woman in red shoes (what a ghastly colour) about Ned. But since the accident, she hadn't been able to think of anything else. How could he have been so careless? Everyone knows you need to wear a hat on a bike. And now he's gone.
>
> How difficult it was, Sara thought, to respond. It wasn't as though she knew this woman. She'd simply come up to her at this rather dreary drinks do, and started to pour out her life story. 'I'm awfully sorry,' she said, looking around, hoping that Hugo would arrive. 'It must be very difficult for you. Now please excuse me. I need to find my fiancé.'

Do you know why this isn't right? I didn't at first. It's because the author is encouraging you to head hop. You have been shown the inside of one person's head and her predicament but before you have a chance to get into their skin, you are suddenly ushered into someone else's. And as a result, it doesn't work. At least, I don't think it does because it isn't realistic enough.

However, it would work if you spent a couple of pages or even a chapter on Marianne and her feelings and what she does next (go on holiday to take her mind off Ned? Contact the woman he had asked her to if anything happened to him?) This would give us a chance to get to know her and sympathise with her situation.

Then, after a decent pause, we could go onto Sara and her new fiancé. And – this is the crucial bit – you create that decent pause by making her become a new chapter OR introducing a line of stars as a demarcation; a way of saying that you are changing gear and getting into someone else's head now.

My novels, as I've said before, are multi-character viewpoint novels. So each character is clearly defined by the chapter they are in. Chapter 1 of *The Wedding Party* is told from Becky's point of view. Chapter 2, from Helen's. Chapter 3 from Mel's. Chapter 4 from Janie's. And then Chapter 5 from Becky's point of view again.

However, you can still see what the other characters are like no matter what the viewpoint. For example, in Chapter 2, Helen receives a phone call from her daughter Becky who is clearly flummoxed. And although the chapter is told from Helen's point of view (or shoes), we gain an insight into Becky who is a harassed mum, trying to cope with a taxing job and the realisation that her father is moving on in life.

> *To understand viewpoint, pretend that you are an alien with the ability to hop into different bodies at a minute's notice. Suddenly you can understand why someone is supposedly 'difficult' or 'fussy' or 'unhappy' or 'apprehensive'. You can see things that only they can see and that no one else can. It's magic!*

Student from one of my writing classes.

Here is an extract from Chapter 2:

CHAPTER TWO

Helen

Helen was planting late tulip bulbs in her head when the mobile rang. It was a trick of hers in spring. They'd come out in early summer when everyone else's had long flowered and faded away so people would say 'Oooh, aren't you lucky that you've still got yours.'

Normally, she'd start planting her second wave in January but with one thing or another, it had slipped her mind. Was it too late? Maybe not with the weather behaving as oddly as it had been. Blast, there it was again. Even if she wasn't driving, her mobile always rang when it was least convenient. Usually, she'd be on her hands and knees and then have to wipe her muddy hands on the side of her jeans in order to prise the wretched thing open.

One day, she promised herself, swerving into a lay-by causing the lorry behind to hoot angrily, she'd get a new mobile which she could flick open one-handed without dropping her trowel. Maybe one of those blue tooths that her son-in-law Steve kept going on about.

It was all very well entering the Age of the Panty Liner but that didn't mean she couldn't keep up with other things.

'Hello?'

The person at the other end was gabbling so fast that if it weren't for the distinctive excited tone, she might have just shoved the phone in her jeans pocket and got on with her mental bulb planting.

'Becky? How lovely to hear from you, darling.'

'Dad'sgettingmarriedagain.'

For a minute, Helen thought her daughter was saying 'Dad's getting buried again'. Her daughter had always spoken fast, ever since she'd been a little girl. The health visitor had said it was because of Adam, her articulate older brother who always dominated the conversation.

Helen's little van rattled as another large lorry shot by. 'Slow down, darling and say it again.'

'I am slowing down. You should have heard me the first time.'

'Well, I thought you said Dad was getting buried again.' She heard herself give a small nervous laugh. 'But that couldn't have been right.'

'Don't be stupid, mum. I said Dad's getting married again. To some woman called Monique whom he met through work. Do you know about her?'

EXERCISE

Write a page from the point of view of one person whom you know in real life. It could be a child or a partner or someone you work with. For instance, you might write something from the point of view of a teenager who has fallen out with her mother. Write it as though that teenager was arguing her case. You might start with the words 'My mother is being totally unreasonable because she won't let me go on holiday with my friends.' Then carry on, as though you are the teenager, who feels she should be allowed to go.

Now write a row of stars or turn over the page. This is to separate the viewpoints. Then I would like you to write another page from the point of view of someone else you know who also knows the teenager. It might be a teacher. Or it could be a friend of the teenager. Hopefully their views will be different and will also show the teenager and mother in a different light.

However, both have the same subjects – the teenager and mother. But they will be from different viewpoints ▨

Benefits of this exercise

Because the two viewpoints are so different, they will show you how important it is to separate viewpoints by stars or chapter breaks. Otherwise the reader can get confused on who is thinking what.

It might also help you develop your character in a more rounded way. Looking at the same character from the point of view of two or three others might make you think of doing something different to them. For instance, in the above exercise, the teacher might mention that the teenager has recently been suspended from school. You might not have thought about this development if you hadn't included a teacher's viewpoint.

EXERCISE

Think about the last argument you had with someone. Write three paragraphs from your point of view, explaining why you were so upset. But don't do it in the first person: give yourself a character's name. Now write three paragraphs from the point of view of the person you had the argument with ▨

Benefits of this exercise

Again, it will help you see the character as a more rounded person as well as the importance of separating viewpoint.

FIRST PERSON, THIRD PERSON OR OMNISCIENT NARRATOR?

I'm often asked by students whether it's best to write in the first person, third or omniscient narrator.

Just to be clear, the 'first person' means writing as 'I'. It tells the story from the viewpoint of the main character who acts as though they are the narrator. For example '*I limped down the road.*'

The third person is when the story is being told from the point of view of an outside character. For example '*Julia limped down the road*'.

The omniscient narrator is when the story is being told from the point of view of a storyteller. For example: '*One day, Julia limped down the road.*'

This is quite a simple way of putting it but there will be several other examples in the chapter.

First person

The big advantage for some writers, about writing in the first person, is that it's easy to get into. For some reason, we all find it easier to pretend that the person we are trying to create is us. By putting 'I' in it, the words can flow more easily, depending on the kind of writer you are. The reader too spots the 'I' and feels at home. Therefore he or she will feel more relaxed.

Another advantage is that the 'I' can allow you to play tricks on your reader. You can hide things from him such as who you really are as a person or who someone else is. This is because you are not honour bound to tell the reader everything. The 'I' is a subjective viewpoint. If you don't wish to tell the reader that Geoff is really a bigamist, you don't have to until you choose. Why? Because no one else is going to reveal it as you are in charge of the story with your 'I'.

You can also mislead the reader with the unreliable narrator technique. For instance, you might claim that the 'I' person is really a young woman but in reality, as the reader finds out at the end, it is an old lady telling her life story.

Personally, I find this kind of twist with the 'I' easier if it's a short story. This is because you can maintain the pretence more easily with a page than with a novel. For instance, I often tell a short story in the first person, pretending that I am a man but am really a woman (or vice versa).This would be more difficult with a novel.

First person and viewpoint
However, there is a school of thought that says that if you write a novel in the first person, your viewpoint is limited. Why? Because if it's 'I, I, I', you can't act as an overall narrator or puppeteer who can see into other people's heads.

Take the following paragraph.

As I got onto the bus, I could see a large woman with a red hat at the front. She looked as though she was going somewhere important. I also couldn't help thinking that I had seen her before. But where? That was it. She had been at a creative writing talk I had gone to in Winchester the other week. She'd seemed rather jolly actually although she was always asking questions.

We get some sort of picture here of the person who is speaking, don't we? And we do get a glimpse of the woman in the red hat. But we can't see what she is thinking because the 'I' person can't just leap into her head in the way that a storyteller could.

But there are ways around it. For instance, the 'I' person could imagine things about the woman in the red hat.

'I could just imagine the kind of person that Adelaide (I seem to recall that was her name) was like outside a writing class. She'd be the sort of woman who would always keep the manual for a new electric appliance. And she'd never stop talking. "My dream," she told the rest of the class, "is to have a job on a remote island in the middle of the Pacific".

As if she would cope on a desert island! She'd need someone to talk to!'

How have we seen into Adelaide's head? Through the use of a simple phrase:

'I could just imagine . . .'

By doing that, you are allowing yourself to peep through the keyhole of someone else's existence. You describe it in such a way that the reader feels they are really there, right next to Adelaide as she triumphantly finds the manual to her boiler when it breaks down. You are there with her, on that island in the Pacific as she stretches out on the white sands. And yet you aren't breaking any rules because the viewpoint is consistent. We are still seeing Adelaide through the 'I' eyes.

The second way we are doing this is through dialogue. Adelaide speaks in that 'I' passage. And there's nothing wrong with that.

She is telling the rest of the class about her island in the Pacific and because it's in speech marks, it seems very realistic. We can picture ourselves right there.

Write a page in the first person (using 'I') and refer to another character in it. Through using phrases like 'I could just imagine' or 'I wondered if. . .', bring in some detail about the other character. But always remember that you are standing in the 'I' shoes ▮

Third person

There are two types of third person. One is where you are sitting on the shoulder of someone so you are describing them very close at hand. And there is one where you are watching them from the stalls of the theatre, several rows away.

The first kind of third person has the advantage of making you feel that you are quite close to that character. I write most of my books in the close third person. Here is an example from the point of view of Janie, a dyslexic wedding planner in *The Wedding Party*.

'What time is the flight?'

Janie glanced down at her list, trying to make sense of the figures. '18.00 hours. They only have to be there two hours before with these tickets because. . .'

'18.00 hours!' Linda screamed, her blue vein standing out in the middle of her forehead. The stress vein, Janie called it. It always sprang to attention in an emergency or a potential disaster.'But that's six o'clock.They'll need to be picked up by 4pm at the latest which means they're going to miss most of their wedding reception.'

Janie felt a cold prickle of fear.Why did people have to use a 24 hour clock? It was so confusing.What was wrong with saying 6pm instead of 18.00 which made you think of 8pm. And why couldn't she remember that 'recepshun' was actually spelt 'reception'?

'I'm sorry. I honestly don't know how that happened. Look, I'll re-book the taxi and . . .'

Linda's vein threatened to burst its banks.'But what about missing their wedding party? What kind of start is that going to be to their married life, let alone the impact on our business?'

Her fists were clenched so tightly that for a moment, Janie felt in danger of being assaulted.'Look, I'm sorry.' The words seemed woolly as they came out of her mouth. Confrontation always did that to her.'It's my mistake. At least, I think it was. Let me just check the airline hadn't changed the flight at the last minute in which case we could claim compensation and . . .'

Linda was so close now she could smell the mouthwash on her breath. 'There won't be any compensation either for us or for you. Because it was your mistake.You're fired, Janie. And don't expect any references.'

Here, we get into Janie's head so we feel quite close to her. We are hopefully concerned for her future.

A helpful piece of advice

Having trouble getting into the close third person? Then tell it in the first person and simply change it to the third. It can allow you to get into that character's skin. Here is an example.

I couldn't help feeling cross that the bus was going to be late. Of all the days to happen! I was going to be late for an interview that had taken weeks to get. And now they'd probably dismiss me as unreliable.

Now change to the third person.

Janie couldn't help feeling cross that the bus was late. Of all the days to happen! She was going to be late for an interview that had taken weeks to get. And now they'd probably dismiss her as unreliable.

Sounds quite authentic, doesn't it?

Far-off third person
The advantage of a far-off third person is that you can use that technique to become an overall story teller. Remember the stories of our youth which used to begin 'Once upon a time, there was an old lady who desperately wanted grandchildren. She did everything she could to persuade her daughter-in-law to get pregnant but to no avail. So one day she...'

This is the omniscient narrator. The story teller. The distant third person. And it has another advantage too. It allows you to confuse your viewpoint a bit more because, as the overall narrator or puppeteer, she can head hop. She can see what's inside the grandmother's head and move on to the daughter's in the next paragraph without having to create that space on the page.

For instance, the next paragraph might read:

'Annie, her daughter-in-law, felt differently. Maureen was an interfering old bag and had no right to present her with fertility charts on the first of every month.'

Why can the overall narrator break the rules? Because we are aware that the narrator is there so we don't feel we have to pretend we are Maureen or even Annie. We know that this is a story because the narrator's voice is strong enough to remind us that, intriguing as the story is, it is only that. A story. It's not real in the same way that we try to make our readers feel as though they are really Becky or Helen or Mel or Janie, depending which chapter it is.

There's another plus about the overall narrator too. And that is that they can become a character in their own right. Fay Weldon has done this very successfully and so has Anne Tyler. They create narrators whose own personality shines through every now and then to remind us that the person telling the story has a life of his or her own. Another example, in a different medium from books, is *Desperate Housewives*. Those of you not familiar with the TV series could do well to study it! The dramatic action is punctuated by a backdrop of commentary – often acerbic, funny and sad at different times – telling us what is happening and what might happen in the future. In fact, the narrator has her own tale to tell which comes out in flashes.

EXERCISE

Write a page in the first person.

Then put it into the third person.

Then tell it from the point of view of someone who is telling the story. In other words, tell it from the point of view of the storyteller

TIP

You can try this exercise with a piece of your own. Or take a page of text from a published novel and use a different viewpoint. For instance, if the story is being told from the point of view of a character called Molly, re-write that page using 'I' and pretending that you are Molly. Then write it again, as though you are a storyteller telling a tale about Molly from a distance. ('Once upon a time, there was a young girl called Molly', etc).

EXERCISE

This one is best done in pairs – it's a good exercise for a writing class.

Pretend you are a famous person but don't tell anyone who you are. Write a page from that person's point of view without mentioning your name. For instance, if you are Elizabeth I, you might start off by saying 'Who says that monarchs have to be men?'. Then you could write a page on why women need to be strong leaders.

Read your work out loud and see if the rest of the class can guess who you are. This isn't just a variation on charades. It will also help you get into your character's head AND see the world from their viewpoint ■

COMBINING PLOT AND VIEWPOINT

Plot and viewpoint go hand in hand. In order for a story to work, you need to see it through the right pair of eyes. Sometimes it's difficult to see whose eyes you should see it through. So the following story and exercise might help.

The other week, when I was walking my dog, I came across a very distressed girl looking for her border collie. He had run off and she'd been searching for him for the last hour. My own dog is quite lively and apt to run off so I felt really sorry for her. So I said I would go in one direction to help find him while she covered another area. I took her number in case I found her collie.

Despite looking everywhere, I couldn't find the missing hound. My search also made me late for an appointment, which made me a little flustered. On top of that, I was worried about the missing dog, especially as the girl's mobile was off when I rang to see if she had found him. I mentioned the girl and her collie to some of my other dogwalking friends in case they came across a stray. But no one did.

Then, three weeks later, I met the girl again in the park – this time with her dog! I wasn't even sure if it WAS her until I asked and then she explained that she had indeed found her collie after a few hours. A man had rung her on his way to work; he had noticed a dog wandering the streets and taken the time to stop him and ring the number on his collar.

The girl was grateful that I had tried to help and we stood and chatted for a while, allowing our dogs to play.

On my way home, it struck me that this might be the germ of an idea for a plot-pusher; a name for an event which moves the plot on in a novel. The idea is not that unusual but if you look at it in a different way, it could provide a twist. Supposing, for example, I wrote it from the point of view of the man who found the dog. Maybe he had just had a row with his wife and left the house early. He dawdles on his way down to the station, feeling bad about the argument and then sees the dog. He rings the number on the dog collar and goes to meet the girl to return her dog.

However, his wife drives past at that moment and sees the two of them together, putting two and two together and making five . . .

I'm not entirely sure what I would write next but it would certainly bring some tension to the plot.

On the other hand, we could also see this story from the point of view of the girl who lost her dog. Maybe it isn't her own dog. Perhaps she is looking after it for a neighbour. Or maybe she's a dog walker. And we could tell the story from the point of view from the woman (me) who tried to help her. Maybe that woman was lonely and had just moved to a new town. Perhaps the girl with the lost dog then becomes a friend.

Isn't it amazing how you can get the germ of a plot as well as lots of different viewpoints from a small, everyday incident?

EXERCISE

Start writing a scene from the first person viewpoint of the man who found the dog or the girl who lost it or the woman who tried to help. If you're doing the man, begin with the words: '*I was half way down the high street when I saw the dog.*'

If you're choosing the girl's viewpoint, begin with: '*I only took my eyes off Rover for a minute before realising he had gone.*'

If you're choosing the woman, begin with: '*The girl in the park was clearly upset.*'

Now see where it takes you. You might find you have a story forming on the page in front of you. Or you might just have fun playing around with different points of view ■

SUMMARY

- Viewpoint is essential! If you get confused, ask yourself whose shoes you are standing in while seeing the story.

- Tell your story from the point of view of one person at a time. If you switch to another person's viewpoint, make it clear through a space on the page or a new chapter.

- If you find it hard to get into the third person, write the passage in the first person and then change it to the third by substituting a character's name for 'I'.

- Use real-life incidents to help.

> *It's a good idea to read some excellent novels – not just for the story but to see how they are laid out. Every writer has a different method. Draw some sense from these examples. That's how I did it myself. See where the paragraphs come and where they begin and end and how to make them more interesting. Make that book your tutor.*
>
> *Also keep at it. Get on with it. Think ahead about where it's going to go. Make sure every scrap of dialogue has a meaning and isn't just trivial backchat. Be very careful not to put too much description in one lump. Pace yourself – don't put everything in the first chapter. Make notes as you go along to add to the plot (I tend to write notes all over the place!).*
>
> *It's a good thing to keep a diary and write down all the dates of things that happen so you can keep the storyline consistent. Include the character's date of birth and future events that characters have referred to. Then you won't forget to include them.*

Elizabeth Lord, author of 20 novels including *Give Me Tomorrow*, Piatkus.

9

De-mystifying Dialogue

Dialogue! In my experience, students either love it or loathe it – which often leads to two things – too much or too little.

TOO MUCH DIALOGUE?

If you have too much dialogue, your novel is in danger of ending up like a script. I've seen all too many students doing this. They have pages and pages of people talking and what they are saying is all good stuff. Except that there's something missing. Their own thoughts inside their heads and also the actions and movements that people always make when they're talking.

Try this as an exercise. Next time you are talking to someone, write down what you are doing as you talk. This might be tricky so only do it with someone you know well! Also give it a whirl while you're on the phone. I know that when I'm speaking to people, I will often multi-task. I can easily empty the bins/unload the dishwasher/clean the kitchen floor while having a conversation. If you make your character do this, he or she is going to seem much more real as a person especially if she drops the bin or her favourite plate from the dishwasher or slips on the kitchen floor – all because they're trying to talk at the same time!

I'd like you to do another exercise too. When you're talking to someone, think about what you're thinking in your head at the same time. It might be '*What a bore this man is?*' or '*Why doesn't she stop talking?'* Then use these inner thoughts when you write dialogue for your character. Maybe it might go something like this:

Polly wedged the phone between her shoulder and ear as she unloaded the dishwasher. 'So I told her,' her mother was saying at the other end. 'I told her that if she did that again, I would complain.'

You don't say, thought Polly. Her mother excelled at complaining. 'You don't think you're slightly over-reacting, Mum, do you?'

Bracing herself, she waited for the inevitable reply...

Do you see how the extra bits (the action and the thought) make that dialogue more interesting?

EXERCISE

Write a conversation between a mother and a daughter or a mother and son. Make sure they are having some kind of disagreement. Include actions and thought ▮

TOO LITTLE DIALOGUE?

Then of course, there's the other side of the coin. Just as some people can't stop talking, others find it hard to get going. The problem with that is that in today's publishing world, editors like dialogue. 'It makes readers feel safe,' one told me recently. 'They see white space around the lines and they don't feel it's as much of a challenge as a page which has lots of text on it. Similarly, they read someone speaking and they feel they are there. They can imagine the scene better and they feel more confident about reading on.'

So how much dialogue should you put in? Some editors suggest as much as 65–70 per cent, which means it's crucial to make it sound right. Many publishers also like dialogue to start by the end of page 1, if not before, because it can draw the reader in. It can be an effective way of starting a chapter too – but only if it's not too vague. If we reach the bottom of the first page and we still don't know who the characters are or where they are or what their relationship is with each other, we could lose interest. So 'root' your dialogue. Make the connections clear. Here's an example from *The Wedding Party.* None of the characters have been introduced before so the reader is as unfamiliar with them as you are:

Mel fiddled with her Portabello Road turquoise drop earrings – she always wore the largest and brightest she could find to cheer up her 'uniform' even though it was a jeans day today – and stared blankly at her empty computer screen.

'Anyone for Afters?' was going to be hard to beat. When she'd first thought of catchy signs outside St Mary's to draw in passing trade, the rural dean had been sceptical.

'I'm not entirely certain of the wisdom, Melanie,' he'd said, sucking his breath in through his two missing teeth and disapprovingly eyeing her second-hand, high-heeled black suede boots underneath her cassock, (she'd come straight from a funeral and hadn't had time to change). 'I agree we need to be part of the modern world but there's a danger, don't you think, of becoming gimmicky like certain other members of our flock.'

'I disagree,' Mel fought an overwhelming urge to nip out for a cigarette. The rural dean always did that to her, even though she'd given up five years ago. 'It's not gimmicky. It's a USP.'

He frowned.'I beg your pardon?'

'Sorry. It's advertising speak for Unique Selling Point.' Swiftly, Mel drew out
a sheet of paper from her briefcase.'These are the attendance figures for
the past five years. You'll see that since I arrived last summer, it has gone up
by ten per cent. I want to improve that but I can only do so with your help.'

There had been a brief silence during which Mel could imagine the rural
dean wondering – not for the first time – why he'd appointed a blonde
mother of two in her mid forties who had come somewhat late to the
church after a varied career in advertising – to be vicar of a traditional
establishment like St Mary's.

HOW TO MAKE DIALOGUE SOUND NATURAL

Sometimes, dialogue can come out so awkwardly that it's like
listening to an amateur script for a school play! Here are some
tips on how to make it flow:

◆ Avoid words like 'Oh' and 'Well' at the beginning of the
sentence.

◆ Make sure your dialogue actually says something instead of
bumbling along about something trivial such as the weather.
Dialogue should act as a plot-pusher. It should frequently tell
the reader or the character something about the story or plot
that they didn't know before.

◆ Use dialogue to develop the character. If you have someone
who is very fussy or worried, you can show this in the dialogue.
Here's an example

'What's wrong?' asked Graham.

Angela frowned as she peered through the curtains. 'I'm sure I heard something out there.'

'Rubbish.' Graham opened a tin of baked beans with a rusty opener that, in his view, should have been chucked years ago. 'You're always hearing things.'

I've just made up this piece of dialogue for the purpose of this section but I think it achieves two things. Both Angela and Graham's dialogue shows that Angela is a persistent worrier. But it also builds up tension. Supposing she has cause for worry this time? Supposing there really is someone out there?

TIP

Try sandwiching dialogue with action and then dialogue. Look at the paragraph above, starting with 'Rubbish.' This is Graham speaking. Now he's opening a tin. Now he's saying something again. It makes a more interesting variation to do this rather than getting a character to speak and then adding 'Graham said'.

I say, I say

On that point, you don't need – in my opinion – to keep having 'she said' or 'he said' or 'Graham said' or 'Angela said'. There is a school of thought that says it's all right to do this because the reader gets so used to it that it ceases to become annoying. I disagree. In fact, I think it looks amateurish. If you make sure that you have a different voice for each character, that should come across in the dialogue and, as a result, your character will be clear.

I suspect, for instance, that Graham is a bit of a bully or at least, he puts Angela down. You could elaborate on this with future dialogue, e.g. '*You really must learn to stop worrying,*' he continued, settling down on the sofa with a cup of tea. '*It's not an attractive habit in a woman.*'

Now we've set the scene, we could have future dialogue without immediately saying who is speaking because the reader will know, by now, that if it's a character who is worrying about something, it might be Angela. And if it's someone who is being dismissive, it might be Graham.

'*I know you think I'm making a fuss but...*'

'*What is it now?*'

No need here, to say who is who. Don't you agree?

   ❛ *I love writing dialogue – in fact, I know a new book has truly has wings when the characters start to hold conversations in my head even when I'm not writing, so that I have to go and scribble them down. And I can hear them doing it – which leads me to my point, a very obvious one: read all your dialogue aloud! It's the easiest way to see if it sounds natural or stilted, or if you have put the punctuation in the wrong place and/or used too many adverbs.*

Another thing you will notice is that very often you don't actually need to say who is speaking, because it is obvious. This especially applies to scenes when only two characters are present, where they will tend to take it in turns to speak. You don't want to sound like a Janet and John reader, do you?

And the dialogue itself will give the tone of the remark, making the addition of an adverb to qualify it redundant. For example, if you have an exclamation mark at the end of a sentence of dialogue, then you certainly don't need 'she exclaimed' after it!

When it comes to viewpoint, I generally write in first person, changing from past to present tense depending on whether my heroine is talking about something that has *happened, or is happening right that minute. Mainly, it is past tense because that is how we tend to evaluate what is happening to us. And when I'm writing in first person, then I become that person for the duration of the novel. That's the fun bit, becoming someone who is totally different to myself, seeing things through their eyes and making choices, right or wrong, that* I *wouldn't have made.*

Usually I also introduce some form of third person viewpoint in one form or another, like Alys Blezzard's journal in my novel A Winter's Tale, *or Josie's articles about Green Living for Skint Old Northern Woman Magazine in* Wedding Tiers.

There are lots of pitfalls to writing a novel in first person and I really wouldn't recommend it for your first novel. But if you are determined on it, then do write in past tense. You need to be a novelist with the technical brilliance of Sophie Kinsella to carry off an entire book in the present tense. In the Shopaholic *books she makes it look so easy and yet it is extremely hard to keep it consistent throughout.*

Trisha Ashley, author of 13 novels including *Sowing Secrets*, *A Winter's Tale* and *Wedding Tiers*, all published by Avon, HarperCollins.

SHOW AND DON'T TELL

Dialogue is a great way of showing and not telling. 'Showing and not telling' means showing how a character is feeling or what they are doing, instead of being told about them at a distance by a story teller or an overall narrator. For instance, if I said 'Angela is a neurotic woman', I would be 'telling' you that. But if I said 'Angela was always thinking that there were people out there to get her,' I would be giving you an illustration of the 'telling' statement and that would be showing.

Dialogue is a good way of showing and not telling because you can include the illustrations in the speech. Here's an example:

'It's no good.' Angela stood up and pulled open the curtains so forcefully that they fell off their hooks.

'Now look what you've done!'

'I knew it!' Angela peered through the condensation on the glass. 'Something's moving in the grass out there. Look!'

I'm beginning to worry myself now! But if this scene had just been 'told', it wouldn't have been so effective. This is how it might have sounded.

Angela continued to worry all evening even though Geoff told her she was fussing unnecessarily. Finally, she stood up and pulled open the curtains. 'There,' she said. 'I can see something moving.'

There is some dialogue in that but not as much as in the first example. And I know which one seems more realistic to me.

(For more on 'Showing and not telling', see Chapter 11.)

ACCENTS

An accent can be a great way of making a character stand out. It could be any nationality or any regional accent – but the crucial thing is that it has to be authentic. If you suddenly decide to make one of your characters Scottish but don't really know much about how a Scottish person speaks, you're on to shaky ground. Because there will be plenty of Scottish people who will read your dialogue and dismiss it as being artificial and not authentic. And as a result, they may be put off reading your book or any others that you write!

If you are determined to include accent, find an expert who can check your dialogue. My Canadian editor did this for me when I had an American character. Yes – I know America and Canada are very different but she still knew more about that than me. And there are certain words in English that mean very different things in America.

Another problem with accents is how far you can go. If you have an Irish character, have you got to make that person's dialogue consistently Irish? That can be quite a commitment and it doesn't always sound natural. One way of getting round this is to start with the Irish dialogue and then, every now and then, remind your reader that the character comes from Ireland. You can do this in the speech or you could refer to it. For example:

'Fancy a pint?' asked Geoff.

Shamus winked. 'And when did an Irishman ever turn down the offer of a free drink?'

Yes, I know this is a cliché but I hope it's made the point!

GRAMMAR

Many of my students get very confused about grammar in dialogue. So here are some basic rules.

Speech marks should normally be double like this: ". However, this depends on the publisher's style – some favour single marks like: '.

The benefit of the double ", is that you can include two sets of dialogue. For instance:

"It's odd," said Geoff. "Our neighbour clearly said 'There's no one in that house' when I spoke to him yesterday."

The single speech mark refers to the words that the neighbour said, to distinguish it from Geoff's speech.

Another rule is that if there's going to be a 'he said', the speech bit should have a comma after it and then the speech marks before the 'said Geoff'. You don't have a full stop because the 'said Geoff' is still part of the sentence. And the speech marks come after the comma. One way of remembering this is to think of the speech marks like a pair of mother's arms, tucking the comma up in bed.

If however, you don't have the 'said Geoff', it would look like this. 'It's odd.' That's because it really is the end of the sentence.

Always remember to start a new paragraph when someone is speaking. It is essential to do this to divide it from someone's thought or speech below. Let's go back to the Irishman. If we didn't have a new paragraph, it would look like this:

'Fancy a pint?' asked Geoff. Shamus winked. 'And when did an Irishman ever turn down the offer of a free drink?'

It's not as clear, is it?

EXERCISE

Write a page of dialogue between two people. One is trying to give the other some good or bad news. It's up to you to choose which. Make sure you:

◆ Include action with your dialogue: maybe someone is drinking a glass of wine or tapping the table with their fingers.

◆ Use dialogue which fits the character. Perhaps the character has a phrase they are always using such as 'Mustn't grumble'.

◆ Don't waste the dialogue on information that isn't needed. Instead, use it to further the plot. For example, a sister might tell her older sister that she can't come on holiday after all because she has to have a serious operation.

◆ Tease the information out so that you don't waste the drama. For instance, the younger sister might just say she doesn't want to go on holiday at first as she doesn't want to worry her older sister about the op. But then, when the other sister gets upset about the cancelled holiday, she tells the truth.

◆ Use a different paragraph every time someone speaks. Make sure the full stop is inside the speech mark■

SUMMARY

◆ Today's contemporary novel has a lot of dialogue – it can be as much as 65–70 per cent.

◆ Don't just rely on dialogue. Include action and internal feelings.

◆ Use the dialogue to push the plot along.

◆ Make sure the dialogue shows and not tells.

◆ Remember grammar rules with dialogue.

◆ Use dialogue to tell the reader something about the character, e.g. someone who fusses or is a bully or is very affectionate.

Do – keep at it! Persistence, no, dogged determination – pay off. In my experience it's the writers who refuse to give up, sometimes after quite severe knock-backs, who make it. Very few just cruise into the writing business and have a bestseller straightaway.

Do – understand that this is an incredibly competitive business. You just need to walk into Waterstones or any other bookshop to understand quite how many other books and authors you're up against. But don't let that put you off. Agents and publishers are always on the lookout for new talent.

Do – take on board any signs, little glimmers of encouragement that you may get in rejection letters. Just because an agent isn't taking you on doesn't mean that your book is rubbish. It may be that they have just taken signed up someone with a very similar profile. Keep trying – your moment will hopefully come.

Do – *be open to constructive criticism. No one's work is perfect and if you keep getting rejection letters, maybe now is the time to re-read your work, reassess, perhaps send it to a book doctor for some advice. I took a whole character out of my first book after a publisher said she felt that there were too many stories going on. At first I was gutted at losing a character that I loved, but once I thought about it, I realised that the publisher was absolutely right.*

Do – *tell people what you're doing. I did! Some don't like to admit that they're writing a novel in case it doesn't come off, but in my experience it reminds you that you're deadly serious about getting published, that it's not just a hobby. And it can act as a bit of a spur and force you to get cracking!*

Do – *think about joining a creative writing group. It helps to talk with other people who are going through the same thing.*

Don't – *show your unpublished work to too many people. Everyone will probably say something different and it will get confusing. Choose one or two respected friends and listen to their views. But remember, at the end of the day it's YOUR book and you can't please everyone. If you don't agree with what they say, have faith in yourself and stick with it.*

Don't – *spend too long perfecting the first draft. It's dispiriting. Getting it down on paper is really important, then you can go back and spend more time shaping and improving. This is my favourite stage – I find polishing my work much more fun than the hard slog of the first draft.*

Don't – *spend too many hours writing in one day. Writing is exhausting. I find four or five hours a day is plenty. If I spend too long it wipes me out for the following day.*

Emma Burstall, author of *Gym and Slimline* and *Never Close Your Eyes* (Preface).

10

Setting

Where are you now? Sitting at a desk? Reading this on a train? Browsing through a bookshop or in the library? Wherever you are, I'd like you to write down the following:

♦ What can you see?
♦ What colours/noises/smells are there?
♦ Is it hot or cold or in between?
♦ What can you feel? (It might be the texture of a chair.)
♦ What can you see when you look out of the window?

All these things are very important when trying to persuade the reader that what they are reading is in fact real. But it is all too easy for the writer to be so caught up in creating a convincing plot and real-life characters, that we forget about the setting. We forget to show what kind of sitting room they are having an argument in or what sort of bed they are lying in or if they can hear the sound of seagulls or trains or children playing.

Similarly, if a novel is going to be interesting, it's crucial to change the scene fairly frequently or else both the writer and the reader gets bored. Time and time again, I see chapters which are set in one room and, not surprisingly, the pace begins to flag. Imagine being stuck in one room with the same people all the time. It would drive you mad. And it's the same in fiction.

For this reason, it's essential to have an idea for a novel that will take you to different places. This doesn't necessarily mean other countries (more on that below). But your characters should definitely be given the opportunity to go to a party; have a walk in the country; take up waterskiing or go to a big city. This in turn will lead to plot development. They will see something or do something that gives the story a push that wouldn't have happened if they'd stayed in the same place.

TIP

If you feel a chapter is beginning to get boring, make your character (or characters) go somewhere else. It might be for a walk in the park. Or it could be getting them stuck in a lift.

GOING ABROAD

I've read some novels where the writer has felt urged to send his character to Australia. Or maybe Hong Kong. Or somewhere that sounds equally glamorous. The problem is that the writer, in many of these manuscripts, has never been there. We often think we can imagine what it's like from all those travel features we read and travel programmes we watch. But there's no substitute for having breathed and smelt that place for ourselves.

I've been lucky enough to have been to both places and I think I could describe the wonderful bright light that you get in Australia when you wake up in the morning and the cool, sophisticated interior of expensive department stores compared with the colourful markets where you can buy silk dressing gowns for under £15. But I couldn't have got that detail without actually being there myself.

I think the golden rule is not to write about a place unless you've been there. Otherwise, you will get rumbled by someone who has and who will then write in and tell you that it's not like that at all. The upside to this is that it's a great excuse to go travelling! Take up any invitation no matter where. Recently, I went to Tynemouth, which is an amazing town in the north east and we sat by the Tyne, eating fish and chips at night. Perfect. Both for us and my novel. But not long ago, I couldn't have written about it because I hadn't been there.

TIP

Go to places you don't normally go to, just to vary your characters' settings. The local swimming pool, perhaps. A coffee shop so you can observe the décor. The top of a double decker bus (hard to find nowadays).

Cheating

That isn't to say you can't cheat a bit! Remember how I suggested that you cut pictures out of characters from magazines to help you describe them. Do the same with pictures of scenery and build up a portfolio. Collect photographs too and always carry a camera with you so you can freeze that scene on film and then describe it later.

DON'T OVERDO IT!

Some writers get so carried away with the setting, that they go on for paragraph after paragraph, enthusing about a place – or maybe criticising it. They forget that a character is waiting in the wings to go on and perform a piece of action.

The trick is to sandwich setting with action so that the reader can see what is happening but within a certain context. Here's an example from *The Wedding Party* when the heroine (a lady gardener) takes on a job looking after a garden she used to own – but doesn't tell the owner she used to live there.

'He laughed; a nice rich, warm laugh like the home-made onion soup she'd just gulped down from the Thermos in the front of the van. 'If there's one thing I've learned since moving to the country, it's that no one uses their front doors. Another thing is that it's never your house; it's always the name of the previous owner. People keep saying to me: 'Oh, you've bought The Old Rectory, haven't you? The Jenkins' house.'

Helen stiffened. Someone had told him; and if they hadn't, this was surely where she ought to tell him that before the Jenkins and before the Wilsons, it had been her house. Hers and Geoff's. . .

'I don't know where you want to start.' He was striding ahead of her now, pulling on a rather newish-looking Barbour. 'It's all so over-grown. I'm sorry.'

'Don't be. It's what I'm here for.' Her eyes were darting around, greedily, drinking it all in. There was the magnolia which she'd planted to mark their fifth wedding anniversary. And there was the buddleia which the children used to hover over, trying to catch butterflies. How that had spread! But where was the lilac tree? She could hardly ask.

'We've got a pond over there but it's horribly overgrown.'

Helen had a sudden flash of hauling out a drenched six year old Becky ('I was only catching tadpoles, mum').'We'll get to it, in time. How about starting with this border? Those irises need thinning out.'

'Wonderful.' Robin glanced up towards the house and Helen followed his gaze. For a second, she thought she glimpsed a face but then it vanished. 'My wife.' He shifted awkwardly.'She likes to look through the window.'

'Pity it's not warmer or she could come out.'

'I don't think so,' Robin sounded flustered.'She likes to stay inside – at least, she has since she got ill.'

There was an awkward silence. Helen put on her gloves which were stiff with dried mud.'Right, I'll get cracking then, shall I ?'

She waited until he walked back to the house, before kneeling down on the grass and getting out her small fork.'Hello,' she whispered softly.'I'm back.'

TRAWL YOUR MEMORY

It's a strange thing but some of us (myself included) can remember a place from our childhood as clearly as though we were there yesterday. And that's great! Don't be ashamed to use it just because you know it well. On the contrary, it can make a scene come alive.

EXERCISE

Think of a special childhood place. Write a letter to someone, explaining what it was like. Take in the effect it had on your feelings; the colours; the smells; the noises; things that happened to you there. Now think about how you could use that in your own novel ▪

EXERCISE

Do this exercise in pairs. Write a piece of action and dialogue about any subject. But don't include any setting. Then do a swap with your partner. Now put in lots of detail about setting (where it is; colours; smells; noises) in each other's work. It might help you to think of things you hadn't considered before ▪

Collect postcards of places , wherever you go. Pin them on a board over your desk and use them to describe scenes in your novel.

‘ *When I was writing my first novel, I thought I ought to include an exotic location to interest an agent. But when I sent off my first three chapters, the agent asked why I had set it in Spain which added nothing to the plot! It taught me not to paint by numbers. Don't use an exotic place because you think it will provide an attractive background. If the plot is strong enough, you don't have to dress it up. I write contemporary fiction so I write on the basis that I need to know the place inside out. If you don't know the area you're setting the story in, you're in risky water. I recently read a novel where the author clearly didn't understand the location – which happened to be a place I do know myself. It spoilt the authenticity.* ’

Lynne Barrett-Lee, co-author of *Never Say Die* with Melanie Davies. Published by Harper True.

SUMMARY

◆ Use magazine pictures to describe a setting.

◆ Use your memory too.

◆ Include the senses such as colour, noise, smell, taste, texture.

◆ Sandwich setting with action and dialogue.

◆ Don't overdo it on setting so it gets boring.

' *Settings are really important to me. In my romantic comedy,* Molly's Millions, *my heroine wins the lottery and decides to give it all away. She embarks on a journey around the UK in her old VW Beetle and I had enormous fun deciding her route – choosing some of my favourite places like the Yorkshire Dales and the Cotswolds and bringing them to life for my readers. I'm a very visual writer and love describing landscapes and the changing seasons. I also love writing about old houses and sometimes feel that the houses have become characters themselves.* '

Victoria Connelly, author of *Molly's Millions*, Allison & Busby, 2009 and three 'magical romances', published in Germany.

11

How to Show and Not Tell

We've already talked a bit about the importance of showing and not telling. But it's so important that it deserves a chapter of its own.

In a nutshell, we are more likely to make our characters seem real if we describe them to our readers instead of just telling our readers what they are like. This doesn't just apply to their clothes or face. It's what they are like inside too.

Chapter 9 has shown you how to do this in dialogue. But there are other ways of showing and not telling as well.

USE STRONG WORDS AND PHRASES

Instead of saying 'Angela pulled the curtains,' we could say 'Angela yanked the curtains open.' This gives a rush of energy to the sentence which makes the scene more vivid.

Here are some more examples:

'He shut the garden gate behind him.' This is telling. But if he 'slammed the garden gate behind him', we can almost see it falling off its hinges!

'She kissed his cheek.' Again, this is telling. But if she 'pecked' his cheek, we get a feeling that this is a short, sharp action rather than a soft, loving one. And that is showing.

Make a list of powerful alternative words for the following:

Smile   Sing   Run   Walk   Cry

INTERNAL DIALOGUE

Showing what someone is thinking inside their head can also be a great way of showing and not telling. You don't need speech marks for this, by the way. For instance, you might have a character called Geoff who might be feeling irritated by his wife Angela's behaviour. But if you just said 'Geoff felt irritated', that would be showing.

However, consider the following sentence: 'Why was she always like that, Geoff wondered.' I feel this sounds more natural. Do you?

EXERCISE
Put the following sentences into internal dialogue. I've done the first one for you (the 'showing' substitute is in bold).

Jane wished the salesman would go away.

Why wouldn't he just leave, Jane wondered. Couldn't he see she didn't want a new kitchen?

I've added more words here but it sounds more realistic. Now over to you!

◆ Jack didn't want any more dinner.
◆ Sally felt hungry.
◆ Lucy was late for work.
◆ William couldn't be bothered to make his bed.
◆ Giles was short of cash

DOCTOR, DOCTOR!

Another way of showing what your character feels instead of telling, is to describe their physical symptoms. I call this the 'Doctor, doctor' method. You pretend that your character is telling the doctor how he or she feels.

Let's pretend that Angela is tired. But instead of writing 'Angela was tired' (which would be telling), we picture her describing her 'tired' symptoms to the doctor. 'My eyes are always heavy and I can't stop yawning,' she said.

Perfect! We haven't even used the word 'tired' but we've managed to show that she is exactly that.

EXERCISE

Consider the following feelings and imagine that your character is describing them to a doctor. I've done the first one for you.

Shaun was happy.

Shaun felt as though his heart had turned into a lovely, warm hot water bottle with a soft cover around it.

This is rather a nice image, don't you think?

Now over to you.

- ◆ Nancy was excited.
- ◆ Michael was being particularly forgetful.
- ◆ James was scared.
- ◆ Susan was annoyed

DOUBLE-CHECKING!

Showing and not telling is so important that I want to give you some more examples.

John is a negative man.

That's me *telling* you that John is sad.

Here's another sentence.

If anyone asked John how he was, he would spend the next half an hour telling that person about everything that was wrong with his life: the leaking pipe in his bathroom; the plumber that didn't come on time to fix it; the state of the street outside. And so on.

Now this is showing you how negative John is. And I've done it by providing detail inside John's head.

Basically, showing is doing exactly that. It's giving the reader an insight into a person or a situation so that they feel they are there.

EXERCISE

John complained to the woman at the council about the rubbish in the road outside.

This is a 'telling' sentence.

Now write a short piece of dialogue between John and the woman at the council about the rubbish. I think you will find it 'shows' rather than tells because it seems more realistic ▓

WATCH YOUR LANGUAGE!

Use strong language! And I don't mean swearing (although I personally don't see anything wrong with this in small doses, providing it fits the character). By strong language, I mean words that are powerful and have oomph. For example, instead of using the word 'walk', how about 'strode'. This has more character, doesn't it?

EXERCISE

Here's a list of words or phrases that we often use. Think of some stronger alternatives to them that will make us visualise the character or place so that we 'show' rather than 'tell'.

Sleep (example: doze).

Large (example: enormous)

Eat

Talk

Laugh

Sat in the bath

Drove

Argue

GET INSIDE YOUR CHARACTER'S HEAD

We started to do this at the beginning of the chapter but now we're going to do this in more depth. Pick an emotion. Any emotion. Let's say it's 'fear'. Now imagine you are scared. Really scared. What does your body do? Mine starts to shake or maybe sweat . My hands might become clammy. My mouth might go dry.

If I said 'John was scared', that would be telling. But if I said 'John's mouth went dry and he began to shake. A small trickle of sweat ran down his back.' Now this would be showing.

EXERCISE

Here's a list of emotions. Imagine how you would feel if you were experiencing them. Now 'give' them to a character and write a couple of lines about how that character would feel if he or she was experiencing them.

Happy

Apprehensive

Awkward

Nervous

Disbelieving

Shy

Thankful

More ways of getting inside that character's head

Try these for size:

Julia stood for ages at the bus stop.

This is telling. So let's imagine what Julia was thinking inside her head and what she might do as a consequence.

Why was the bus so late? Julia studied the timetable again at the bus stop to make sure she hadn't missed it.

Here's another.

Gary was fed up with his diet. It wasn't working, anyway.

This is 'telling'. But we can make it into a 'showing ' paragraph if we share his frustration.

It was a stupid diet anyway! Gary was blowed if he was going to stick to it any more. Just look at those scales. They hadn't budged an inch. Waste of time! He might as well go out and have a takeaway...

You can see that much of the above paragraph is as though Gary was talking to himself or someone else, justifying why he is giving up his diet. And that's what we need to do in order to 'show'.

And some more
- **Include as many details as possible so the reader feels he/she is there**
  She swallowed her breakfast quickly.
  She wolfed down her bowl of Bran Flakes as fast as she could.

  The dress in the window was just what she'd been looking for.
  The long, red dress with the nipped-in waist would be perfect for the drinks party.

♦ **Use dramatic images**

His words lifted her like a rainbow warming her heart.

His words sliced through her like an old-fashioned cheese cutter.

♦ **Get inside your main character's skin – more ideas!**

Judith was cold as she waited in the biting wind.

It was freezing! Why was Derek late again?

Sally was excited about her holiday.

Sally couldn't wait! All that lovely sun just waiting for her!

SUMMARY

♦ Showing and not telling can be achieved by:

♦ Using strong language

♦ Getting inside a character's head

♦ Using dialogue.

1. Ask yourself: 'Has the novel got the legs?' Is it merely a long short story? But more importantly, has it got the scope? Find the over-riding theme, which should be a fundamental: love, betrayal, jealousy. I wrote a novel about bigamy that sustained itself because at route level I was fascinated by dual-identity (it never saw the light of day because I didn't follow the next strictures).

2. Work as you work. If your routine is 2 hours an hour, do 2. If it's 8 do 8. If you hate reading when you are writing, don't read. If you like to write upside down in the snow with a tuba playing next to you write in the snow, upside down In fact, listen to no one about how to write and what to write and when to write. Overall I think there is too much advice (I'm laying myself as wide open as a barn door here!). There's too much 'education', and a lot of that is the writer's fault because he/she asks for too much advice that, paradoxically, they do not always want to take. However . . .

3. Have 2 or 3 (at most) readers that you trust and keep to their advice/promptings. To me this is just as vital as a producer casting for his film. You trust these people not because they are friends/ relatives but because they come with constructive criticism; are wise; are good readers; are sympathetic to new writers.

4. Have in your 'mind's eye' who you are writing for. Just as a musician on stage sometimes plays for one face in the audience, so you might write for just one person. It works.

5. Let the characters decide. By all means have a plan for your novel if that is the way you work, but be flexible. Even on a subconscious level, the reader sniffs out, for example, the overly neat and tied-up ending. Remember; people are interested in people.

6. It doesn't matter how long it takes to complete your novel including all the re-writes, etc. Some people take all their lives to produce one work of art. Sometimes it kills them yet we, the audience, don't even care about that. What we care about is that they DID IT. Therefore, however long it takes you will have a legacy.

Rob Richardson, creator of WriteInvite.

12

Sense and Sensibility

SMELL

When my first novel *The School Run* was accepted, my new editor said 'We love it but where is the smell?'

And do you know, I'd been so busy concentrating on the characters and plot, that I hadn't mentioned smell – not once! Yet people DO smell, don't they? Hopefully in a nice way although not always. Only yesterday, I walked past a woman in the street very early in the day. She was getting into her car and I was walking my dog. Even from a distance, I could smell that she had just got out of the shower or had liberally overdosed herself with scent – even my dog (who smelt of doggy shampoo) sneezed and I found myself feeling sorry for the people she might be sitting next to in the office. (She was wearing a smart suit so I presumed she might be going to work although, of course, it could be to a wedding or a funeral or a meeting with a lover or an ex – already I'm getting the idea for a plot here!)

But the important lesson is that smell can define a person. It can make that character real in your head. And it can do the same to a place.

The golden rule about smell, however, is not to overdo it like the woman with the shower gel or perfume. If everything you write about has a smell, it can seem forced and artificial. Far better to pepper your sentences every now and then with an allusion. It might be the nutty smell of the trees in autumn. Or it could be the heady smell of lilies. Or it might be the clean smell of a bar of male soap.

It can help too, to be specific. What kind of male soap? Providing you don't defame it (which might lead to legal action), I think it's helpful to say the brand. It all helps to create that picture of reality. I've had characters who smell of Blue Grass because that's a scent my mother used to wear. And if your head is nodding, maybe it's because you can think of a scent that your mother or someone close to you used to love.

COLOUR

These lessons also apply to colour. What colour is the blouse your heroine is wearing? What colour are her eyes? Try to make them different; not the standard blonde hair and blue eyes. How interesting if one eye is brown and the other is green! And does your heroine always wear yellow? If so, why? When she turns up wearing red one day instead, what has happened to her life?

By using colour cleverly, you can develop your plot as well as the whole picture.

SOUND

We've talked about this briefly in characterisation (Chapter 7) when we explored how to make characters sound different. But they need to hear things too. I had a lovely day recently, on the south coast where the over-riding sound was that of seagulls! They screamed; they argued; they chorused; they yelled. They made the world come alive that day – and they could do the same for a line of fiction.

TOUCH

When you buy a new dress or pair of trousers or even t-shirt, do you touch it? I do. I like things that feel nice. And I like the textured feel of my husband's jacket. Your hero or heroine needs to do the same too, if he or she is to be a real person. They might feel itchy from the fabric of a sofa they are sitting on. Or they might hold a piece of material close to their face because the touch reminds them of the feel of their mother's skin.

TASTE

So your characters are having a meal in a little café with red and white checked tablecloths that feel slightly rough when you run your hand over them and shiny silver modern cutlery. They're tucking into a vegetarian lasagne that's been heavily flavoured with garlic and there's the smell of something delicious (crispy roast potatoes?) from the kitchen. We've got colour. We've got texture. We've got smell. And now we need taste. What does the lasagne taste of? Is it cheesy or oniony or is it so hot that it burns the tongue? Maybe it's cold.

By now, you might be loving or loathing the lasagne – but it doesn't matter. The important thing is that we have roped the reader in by including taste.

Keep a 'sense and sensibility' daily diary. Draw three vertical lines and make each one a column for 'smell', 'taste' and 'colour'. At the end of every day, write down all the smells you've encountered that day; all the tastes; and all the colours. If you find them hard to describe, ask yourself what it reminds you of. Maybe the sound of the music on the radio sounds like your vacuum cleaner when it's picked up a nail by mistake and it's got stuck in the hose.

Keep your sense and sensibility diary for a whole week. Use it to refer back to when you need to insert colours, smells and tastes. When you get short, do a diary for another week.

Sophie King

EXERCISE

Make a list of five different sounds that you've heard recently and put them into a sentence. Use power words to make them real. Here's an example.

The car engine roared into action.

Now do the same with colour (the red ruby gleamed); smell (her scent knocked me sideways); touch (I chose the curtains because of the silky feel); taste (semolina always makes me feel sick).

If, by now, you've already written part of a novel, take a page and add some of these sentences■

And another exercise!

EXERCISE

Make a note in your Ideas book of interesting colours. Don't just say something is 'blue'. What kind of blue is it? Peacock blue/sapphire blue/ Quality Street purple?

What kind of smells do we come across every day? Write down a list of your favourite smells to prompt you, e.g. freshly mown grass/favourite perfume. How could this help you make a character come to life?

What food makes your mouth water? Consider how you can incorporate cooking smells into your writing■

TIP

This is something you can add after the first draft. It's difficult to remember to do everything, first time round! But you'll see in the chapter on revision (Chapter 14) that you can then add other layers – and smell, colour, noise, etc are some examples.

SUMMARY

When you've finished your first draft, go back and put in colours, smells, tastes and textures. Be aware of these as you're writing, too.

❝ *First and most importantly, think of an effective title for your novel. Write a plan of the story, for that is what you are telling, and narrative descriptions of your main characters. As you write, things will change and evolve but the prior thought and planning will help you to tell a good tale convincingly and maintain the narrative drive. Try to write for a short time every day, even if it is only for an hour early in the morning, as this enables you to continue creating your book in your head ready for committing it to screen or paper the next day. It also means that you will finish the book in a relatively short time so it does not lose its impetus or freshness or miss the current trends and zeitgeist which inspired it in the first place. Also, read other books in the same category or subject area as your own, ones which have sold well or been bestsellers. Do not be afraid to analyse and deconstruct their title, characters, stories and so on to see what it is that has made them popular.*

In spite of what I have said about trends and zeitgeist, remember that often what goes around comes around and publishers are still looking for 'the new' Rosamunde Pilcher twenty years after the publication of The Shell Seekers *and the next Patrick O'Brian to bring us more seafaring, 'creaking masts' classics from the Napoleonic Wars.*

I have working in my office a very successful young man who has just had his first novel, set in the First World War, published by Faber to impressive critical acclaim. When I asked him for any advice, he just frowned and said 'basically, just do it'. He has a point.

Heather Holden, Brown, agent

13

Humour

Humour is one of those skills which is much more difficult than it looks. But if you can achieve it, you will make your reader feel warm and receptive to your story. In other words, you will hook them – and then you could be on to a winner.

So how do you do it? The best way to be funny is to do it unintentionally. Think of real-life situations where not everyone sets out to be funny but then they do something or say something which is hilarious.

In other words, the humour comes from the character acting in a certain way and/or from a situation which is amusing. Recently, for instance, some friends of ours waited in all day for a delivery of garden furniture from a well-known home improvement store. By 5pm, it hadn't arrived so our friends rang and complained. To their annoyance, the store couldn't find their order but very politely promised to look into the matter. By 6.30pm, our friends were writing a stern complaints letter – and then the delivery van drew up. It was from a rival home improvements firm. The wife had forgotten that although they'd considered furniture from the first, they actually ordered from the second! So when the first store couldn't find their order, it was because it had never been placed.

It's this kind of situational humour that is not only natural but which can also move a plot on in a novel.

Eccentric characters are great at providing humour. I used to work at a smart magazine where one of the employees would wear shorts to work, winter and summer. It certainly made him stand out – and it would also do the same in print.

Lucy's mother-in-law in *The Supper Club* is another example; she's very controlling and insists that a chicken casserole is a vegetarian dish for one of Lucy's guests 'because chicken doesn't count as meat'.

Dialogue is a good way of making humour sound natural, providing it's not forced. I personally find that children's dialogue is particularly good for this. After all, kids do say the funniest things. . .

EXERCISE

Think of something funny that has happened to your or someone you know. Consider how you could use that in a novel ▉

TIP

Children can be great sources of amusement. They often come out with some howlers because they frequently say what they think.

Make a list of all the funny things that your own children or other people's children have said. Then try to weave it into dialogue.

Here are some real-life examples.

'I liked the socks but not very much.'

From a Christmas thank you letter.

'Mummy says it's very annoying that you were late'.

A small child greeting the babysitter.

'I've been sick all night! I told Mummy I didn't feel well but she said she had to go back to work and that you would look after me.'

Six year old telling his teacher when he was sick again in class, after his mother had said he was well enough to go back to school.

'I didn't realise we had a kitchen bin.'

15-year-old boy (who had lived in the house for five years).

Just putting these sentences into dialogue makes us laugh, doesn't it? And there's no need to over-egg it by getting one of the characters to say something like 'That's funny'.

HUMOROUS EXAMPLE

Below is an extract from my first novel, *The School Run*. It's from the point of view of Martine, the French au pair. I'd like you to consider the following when reading it:

♦ Dialogue.
♦ Confusion over language.
♦ Input from children.
♦ Difficult situations.

(The first two lines, by the way, is an announcement on the car radio.)

LONG QUEUES ARE ALREADY BUILDING UP ON THE MARYLEBONE BYPASS, CAUSING SEVERE CONGESTION.

Congestion? What is that? I'll must seek it in the dictionary and engrave it in my vocab book like my tutor said. It is a good tip, n'est ce pas? My tutor, she also say to write this diary. Me, I always engrave in a diary every day even when I am at home. But I do not know if it is aiding my studies. The English language is so strange and the radio speaks so rapid. But je pense it is coming. Last night, I even dreamed a morsel in English. It is a hopeful sign, n'est-ce pas? The reve, distressingly, was not hopeful. I dreamed concerning I was home again. I was lying in a proper bed – these English mattresses are so lumpy – with my bolster instead of these pillows that Sally donates me. The shutters at the window were open and my mama was standing in front of them, calling me to get up.

'C'est petit dejeuner' she is saying. I could smell the coffee – real coffee, not like these granules terrible – and feel the croissants dissolve into flakes in my fingers. And then I wake and find it is me who has to get the children breakfast. No one is there to make breakfast for me any more.

My father, he say my conscience needs to be pricked. He say my rest in England will prick it for me. But my mother, she understands. I am not a bad girl. I just fell in love. In addition, I do have a conscience whatever my father says. Whoever reads this diary will comprehend my conscience but I must take care that no one finds it.

Warning!

Humour can sometimes be quite offensive. So be careful who you poke fun at, even if it is in a 'gentle' way.

'The best humour comes not from thinking 'Wouldn't this be funny if A, B, C happened' but 'wouldn't it be tragic if it wasn't funny if A, B, C happened.'

Also remember that if something is boring you in your own book, there's a strong chance it will bore your reader. '

Simon Brett, writer.

14

Different Genres

What kind of novel are you writing? By now, you might have had a chance to think about it. And maybe this is the time to consider the type of 'genre' you are interested in.

'Genre' is simply a fancy name for the 'type' of book. It might be an historical. Or crime. Or romantic comedy. Or sci-fi.

> ‘ *Don't be afraid to try out different genres. I changed genre recently when I started to write historicals and now I do Regency romances. I'd also advise first time novelists to have lots of patience. Don't expect everything to happen fast. Keep going. If you don't get an agent immediately, keep working at it. You need an element of stubbornness. Believe in yourself and just keep going.*
>
> *Another tip that worked for me before I was published as a novelist is to write short stories. It gave me self-confidence and you can transfer your skills to novel writing. I still write short stories as well as novels.* ’
>
> Jan Jones. Winner of the RNA Joan Hessayon Award in 2005 with *Stage by Stage*. Author of *Fair Deception* and *Fortunate Wager*, both published by Robert Hale.

Below are some pros and cons of each.

HISTORICALS

Pros: popular at the time of going to press.

Cons: you need to know your subject well. That includes understanding how people dress; speak; what they ate, etc during that time.

CONTEMPORARY ROMANTIC FICTION

Pros: you might feel you know something about this yourself. You can bring in your own dramas.

Cons: very competitive market.

CRIME AND THRILLERS

Pros: again, always popular.

Cons: you need to know your subject. Do you understand how fingerprints are taken? This could leave holes in your credibility if you get it wrong.

SCI-FI

Pros: there's a dedicated following out there.

Cons: it's limited. Some agents won't touch it.

EXERCISE

Read a book in a genre that you don't normally touch – with me, it would be sci-fi! It might inspire you ■

' *When an aspiring writer asks me for advice on writing a novel, apart from the first word that comes to mind: "Don't!", I would have to say: take it seriously. There are people who faff about with a novel in progress for, quite literally, years. That means they aren't serious about it. If you are serious, get on and write it. Finish it. That's a huge achievement in itself. Then you can polish, or rewrite, or get on with the next one. But keep writing. It does happen – all of us quoted in this book were unpublished once!'*

Lesley Cookman, author of *Murder in The Green* (sixth in the Libby Sarjeant series), *Murder in Steeple Martin, Murder at The Laurels, Murder in Midwinter, Murder by the Sea, Murder in Bloom.*

15

How to Keep a Timeline

It's incredibly easy when you're so involved with keeping all these balls in the air – characterisation, plot, setting, viewpoint, dialogue, etc - to lose track of time. I'm not talking about how long you've been up in the spare room, writing your novel when the rest of your family is wondering where lunch is (that's another story). I'm talking about the art of ensuring that Tuesday doesn't come after Wednesday in your novel.

Now this might seem obvious but trust me – it isn't. It's an easy mistake to get one of your characters to arrange to meet another in four days' time, the following Wednesday. But somehow, you make another character do something else on the Tuesday and, without thinking, say it took place in five days' time...

The best way round this is to go back to that big book where you've already started to keep a note of what characters you have; what they are like; what they do. Add another section – timing. Write down – ideally on each character's page – what you have promised the reader that that character will do at a certain time. So if you've said that Polly is four months' pregnant, you know that she had to produce by chapter 7, otherwise it's going to be an eleven-month pregnancy!

Timeline is one of those problems that authors think they can skate over without anyone noticing. Even established writers can promise something in the plot (such as a birthday or a holiday) that

*never happens or which takes place at the wrong time. So every time
you say something will happen, write it down in red and then make
sure it happens – when it should do!*

Publisher who didn't want to be named.

SPECIAL OCCASIONS

I've certainly been guilty of starting a novel in the autumn and
then letting a good five months elapse before realising that I have
managed to miss one of the most important special occasions of
the year – Christmas.

But I've only done that in the first draft. I've then gone back and
put Christmas in which often means readjusting the plot. Because
Christmas can change people's relationships. It can make parents
fall out with children. It can prompt young couples to get
engaged. It can encourage others to go away to escape from it all.
In other words, it can 'up the ante' for a plot and create more
interest.

Sometimes, however, Christmas just doesn't fit into the scheme of
things because there's so much going on. This happened in my
novel *The Supper Club* which was set over the months of the year.
However, when it got to the beginning of December, a big crisis
occurred with my characters. That left me with a dilemma. If I
brought in Christmas, it would take the focus away and water
down the crisis. So I did what most of us would do if we had a
big thing to deal with at this time. I got the characters to agree
that it wasn't appropriate to hold the Christmas meal they had
planned and that they would do it in the spring instead.

Here's a list of other special occasions which you need to add to your timeline. You may not use them all but they might need to be acknowledged.

◆ Valentine's Day.

◆ Father's Day.

◆ Mothering Sunday.

◆ The Sabbath and other religious days such as Easter.

◆ Summer holidays.

◆ Bank holidays.

◆ Hallowe'en.

◆ New Year.

SEASONS OF THE YEAR

We've already discussed the importance of colours, smells and other senses as well as setting. In order to make the most out of them and make your novel as realistic as possible, you need to remember to change the seasons in your novel – if the timespan is over a few months.

One easy way of doing this is to go back to your tree diagram where you will have written a list of plot events, usually after you have finished the novel.

Take a look at the branches and work out which season certain events happen in. Then go back to your first draft and add little words or maybe sentences to give a sense of season.

Keep a season's diary all through the year and note down observations so that you can use them in your novel. At the time I am writing this, it's August and the evenings are light. It's slightly muggy during the day and I don't know whether to take a cardigan when I go out. The buddleia is out in full bloom in the garden and every time I pass it, I'm tempted to bend down and smell it. There's a wasp's nest by the back door which I need to sort out.

These are the kind of little details which I may well forget about if I am writing a summer scene in the winter. But if I have a 'season's diary' to refer back to, it will be easier.

COUNTING DOWN THE YEARS

If your novel is set over several years, try this as a way of keeping track and making sure your characters do what they should at the right time.

Draw a vertical line and then a series of notches up the line. Starting with the first notch at the bottom, write the year that your novel starts in. Continue up the line with consecutive years. Now extend those notches into horizontal lines and on them, write down events that you have said, in your novel, took place in those years. Look at the whole picture and check they make sense.

EXERCISE

Study a novel that you have already read. Flick through it and remind yourself what happened. Then write a timeline for it, noting down the different weeks or seasons and big events

Keep a season's diary and write down what it looks like when the leaves fall. Then, when you're writing an autumn scene in summer, you can remember all the little bits you might have forgotten. Don't worry if you haven't got your characters real in the first half of your novel. It will get easier in the second when you will have got to know them better. That way you can go back and fill them in.

Keep a balance between dialogue, description and plot. Don't have too much of one and not the others.

If you get stuck, write a letter to your best friend describing what is happening or going to happen. Then use it instead of posting it.

> Jilly Cooper, novelist (who kindly made time to ring me back and give this quote, specifically for this book).

SUMMARY

- Make a timeline to check your characters do what you've promised at the right time.

- Keep a season's diary.

- Include special occasions in your novel.

16

The Art of Revision

There's a great temptation for writers to finish the last sentence and immediately post it off to an agent before the printer ink is even dry! And why not? Supposing someone else gets there first with your idea?

It's true there is a danger in this. But it's equally true that if an agent reads the first page of your novel and spots a typo or a time mistake or simply doesn't enjoy it, it will get dumped straight in the Reject pile.

Far better to put your novel away for a bit and then come back to it with a fresh eye. It's amazing how much you will then see that needs changing. That first sentence isn't as punchy as you thought but hey – you've thought of something better.

And that's the strange thing about writing – well, one of them. You can be walking along the street or in a shop or doing something totally unconnected with your novel, when you'll suddenly realise that you shouldn't have done such and such with a character; you need to do something else instead. And if you've already sent your manuscript off to an agent, it's too late to ring up and ask if they'd mind changing the third sentence because you've thought of something better. That just looks amateurish. So wait and make sure that you've read through your manuscript before sending it off (for details on that, see Chapter 20 on How to Get Published).

PRINT OUT

It's also essential to do any revision from a printed-out version rather than from the screen. You can miss a lot by just looking at the latter, partly because your eyes may be tired by now. I prefer to print off the whole novel and then read it through. I'll write down changes on the manuscript and then type those on to the screen. Then I'll print off the whole lot again and go through it chapter by chapter.

The changes I make may be to do with plot and believability and characterisations. But I will also add clues to twists (provided they're not obvious) and senses, etc, as well.

TIP

To save paper, print on the other side of something you don't need any more. But don't do it on previous versions of your novel or you might get muddled about which one is the latest version.

READ OUT LOUD

If you have the privacy, it's a good idea to read your novel out loud. This is particularly useful when it comes to dialogue because it helps you to see the voice.

THE RED PEN

Betty Schwartz, who used to handle the slush pile at Hodder & Stoughton and is now a literary consultant, advised me to go through my novel with a red pen and strike out any internal thought after a page (maximum). This, she told me, is because readers like plenty of action and not just pages and pages of internal anguishing. It's been good advice. (More advice from Betty on page 190.)

COMPUTER HASSLES

Make sure you don't delete your revised version by mistake – very easy to do. I clearly mark my file under the name of the first novel followed by 'first draft'; 'second draft' and so on.

And – it goes without saying – always, ALWAYS back up. You can do this easily by sending yourself your novel as an attachment to your own email address. Then, if the house burns down or your computer has a breakdown, you can access your email account from someone else's computer.

Another tip is to send the novel in an attachment to a friend or relative, providing they promise not to open it!

TO CUT OR NOT TO CUT?

My editor has always encouraged me to write 120,000 words rather than 140,000 (which is my natural length). At first, when I had to cut 20,000 words, I was horrified. But then I found that by cutting a few words, it all added up. Then I began to cut bigger sections and ended up with a tighter book. It's like having a hair cut and realising that the old shaggy look didn't suit you the way you had fondly imagined.

Never send out your submission before you're ready! Sit on it. It's very tempting to send out a novel in the heat of the moment, as soon as you have finished – before you've even revised it. Instead, revise; read out loud; out on one side; re-write. Then target your agent. Don't ever blanket submit to agents.

Helen Corner, from Cornerstones Literary Consultancy.

ENJOY IT!

Enjoy this revision time! The story is written. Most of the hard work is done. Now you need to polish so your novel is the very best you can make it. See yourself as a kind of literary hygienist instead of dental hygienist and be proud of your results!

And then pat yourself on the back!

You've finished your novel! This is a fantastic achievement in itself. OK. You don't know at this stage if it's ever going to be published. But you should celebrate – either with others or by yourself – because you have proved that you've been committed enough to get to 100,000 words (or so).

Not everyone can do that. In fact, many people give up before they reach the half way mark.

You will also have learned some important lessons on the way. You'll have found what works for you and what doesn't. Maybe you've discovered that you're great at characterisation but not so hot on plot. Or vice versa.

So take the time now to concentrate on your weak areas. Read other novels and see how the author has done it. Clearly I'm not suggesting copying anything. But you can get some general ideas on technique. Join a good writing class for help with your weak spots. Or consider going to a literary advisory service (see Useful Addresses at the end).

But above all, praise yourself for having reached the finishing line.

Quiet ways to celebrate

◆ Go for a walk.

◆ Have a day out.

◆ Visit a place that helps you unwind (writing is very tiring). I love going to art galleries.

◆ Have a lie in.

◆ See friends again.

◆ Go to a day spa. (I adore Champneys and you can get some great day rates.)

Don't be surprised if...

You've already got an idea for the next novel. This is a good sign. Authors and publishers like to know that a novelist has got lots of ideas up his or her sleeve.

BUT don't be tempted to start writing the next book the day after you finish the previous one. You need time to recuperate and let the imaginative juices flow again. After all, a marathon runner doesn't start to run a new race as soon as he's finished.

I reject countless novels simply because there are typos on the first page. If a would-be author can't be bothered to get it right at the beginning, it doesn't bode well. So check, check, check. Read it silently and then out loud. Don't rush it.

Agent who didn't wish to be named.

17

Synopsis

We've all heard of it but what does it mean, exactly? A synopsis is simply the telling of the story from start to finish without any frills. It means that an agent or publisher can read it and know exactly what happens.

It is NOT a blurb: the words on the back cover which hint at the story outline but don't tell you what happens in the hope you will buy the book to find out.

And because you need to tell the story from start to finish, I personally think it's best to write a synopsis AFTER you have written the novel. Otherwise you are stuck with the predicament of having to write the whole outline before you have allowed the characters to develop.

A synopsis also needs to outline the characters but don't do this as a separate section. Include them in the plot outline. For instance, in *Second Time Lucky*, my synopsis would have said that Louise is a single mother of three who moves, with her teenagers, into an apartment and makes friends with her neighbours. One of her neighbours is Mollie, a retired actress whose husband has died. There's also Marcie, an American bride and Roddie, whose family used to own the large house which has been converted into flats where they all live. Then I would outline what happens to all these characters.

Personally, I don't like synopses (that's how you spell the plural). They're bald and they have to tell rather than show. But I can also see that they are essential if an agent or publisher is to spot the potential of your story.

TIP

Although the rest of your manuscript should be double spaced (see Chapter 20 on how to get published), your synopsis can be single spaced. The good news is that means you can get more words on the page. The bad news is that a synopsis should, ideally, be only one page long.

EXAMPLE

Here is a sample synopsis of my latest novel *The Wedding Party*:

The Wedding Party is a contemporary romantic fiction novel with darker elements. It is the story of four people who are going to a wedding in nine months' time. The novel is told from the point of view of each character so their lives form the focal point of the plot. Through them, we gradually learn about the bride and groom.

Becky is a journalist in her early thirties with two young children and a busy job. She is upset when her father Geoff announces his intention to get married to a woman he has only recently met, called Monique. Becky's reaction makes her examine her own marriage and she embarks on a relationship with someone else. However, when her husband misreads the relationship, they break up for a period and this makes her re-examine her life, as does her redundancy. By the end of the novel, she is reconciled with her husband and has a new career change.

Helen is the groom's ex-wife. She runs her own garden business (both digging and designing) and is dating David who persuades her to get engaged. However, news of her ex-husband's marriage makes her go back to the house they used to own (for old times' sake) and there she meets Robin, the new owner whose wife is in a wheelchair. She agrees to help him out with the garden without telling him she used to own it. Without meaning to, they fall in love and Helen breaks off her engagement. Then Danny, her dog, accidentally pulls the owner's wife into the garden pond and she drowns. Horrified, Helen says she can never see Robin again. However, by the end of the novel, she is persuaded by Mel, the vicar, that the wheelchair accident was not her fault and she ends up with Robin.

Mel is a glamorous vicar who used to be in advertising. She struggles with a redundant husband and two challenging teenagers. Her daughter is knocked over by a hit-and-run driver and is in a coma for most of the novel – this makes Mel struggle with the notion of forgiveness. One of the last people to see the daughter alive was Geoff, the groom, who came to the vicarage to organise his wedding. This makes Mel feel close to him and they are in danger of falling into a relationship. However, by the end, Mel becomes reconciled to her husband and the daughter wakes out of her coma, thanks to her brother's band which plays around her hospital bed.

Janie is a dyslexic wedding planner who frequently gets things wrong. She has been sacked from several jobs but sets up her own business called For Weddings and a Funeral, organising wedding and funeral services with her elderly neighbour Marjorie. Janie finds her boyfriend Mac in bed with someone else so boots him out. She then finds love with Lars, a Scandinavian, whom she meets at a wedding fair, but loses his number. Mac turns up and she is tempted to go back to him. Meanwhile, Janie makes several mistakes when organising Becky's father's wedding. Janie finally ends up with Becky's brother Adam whom she used to know as a child – but not before she makes several more 'cock ups' with the wedding service.

Meanwhile, the bride (Monique) turns out to have had a past which includes a relationship with Adam, the groom's son. She still married Geoff the groom but the reader gets the impression that this might not be a marriage made in heaven.

You can see from this that this synopsis has simply outlined the story without any emotion; hopefully the actions speak for the power behind the events. I could not have written the synopsis before having written the novel, as many of the ideas came to me while I was in the middle of writing it.

It might help, when writing your synopsis, to bear in mind, the following pieces of advice from novelist Bernadine Kennedy author of several novels, including *Shattered Lives*.

Love your characters

Get to know, understand and care about your characters, even the 'bad' ones and make them interesting as it is they who move the storyline along for you. If you're really lucky they sometimes even take over and write the book for you!

The story comes first

Do be careful not to over-edit as you go along, you'll lose the spontaneity and your personal 'voice'. The nitty gritty of factual details, grammar, punctuation and layout can all be dealt with during the editing and polishing at the end.

The most carefully presented manuscript is useless without a good story inside it.

Selling it

The Editor/Agent the manuscript goes to will be looking for a cracking story that catches them on the first page and makes them want to read on; it has to have that certain something that draws them in and doesn't let them go. Make sure yours is it!

Remember that will also be the selling point if it makes it through the process on to the shelves for sale to the public!

18

The Title

The title of a novel is one of the first things that an agent or publisher sees. It needs to be snappy. Punchy. And it needs to be different. It also needs to sum up in a few words, the content of the novel.

Most novel titles are short and snappy. But recently, there have been some exceptions – really long ones which have stood out just because of that. Here's an example:

Guernsey Literary and Potato Peel Pie Society (by Annie Barrows and Mary Ann Shaffer). This novel is about occupied Guernsey, believe it or not.

TIPS ON HOW TO CHOOSE YOUR TITLE

Alliteration helps
If you can think of a title where the words all start with the same letter, you might be on to something. Have a go!

Questions
Readers like something that makes them think. So something with a question mark at the end might also make it stand out.

Secret
Anything with the word 'secret' tends to sell. Most readers love the mystique.

Tell and don't show

Although everyone's been telling you to show and not tell, I think you'll find that titles are the exception. Telling what happens in the story, within the title, can be a way of hooking in the reader – especially if it's a situation they recognise. For instance, my first novel was a great success, partly because its title *The School Run* said exactly what it is about. And it was – is – a subject that people are constantly caught up in, either because they're on it themselves or because they are stuck behind a school-run car.

Check the competition

There are books around with the same title. But I personally think it's best to be different.

How to check out your idea

Write out your titles and put them up on cards round the house. It gives you time to look at them visually. Ask other readers what they think. And find a friendly bookstore manager or seller to give you feedback. Also wander round bookshops and look at the top 50 bestsellers. What kind of titles do they have? Why do they work for you – or why don't they?

EXERCISE

Think about the novel you want to write or are writing, and come up with five different titles.

Pick one of your favourite books and give it a different title.

Go to the local bookshop and library. Pick out books where the titles leap off the shelves. Ask yourself why they work. What can you learn from that? ■

❛ *Firstly, concentrate on the story. Whose story is it? Which of your characters drives the narrative? What is the underlying moral of the tale? Does good triumph over evil – World War II story about the French resistance? Will the truth always out – court room drama/detective story? Will love conquer all – romance? Once you've got your characters and underlying premise just write from the heart.*

The bread pudding in the middle

There is a point in any story, somewhere between chapter eight and twelve, when you've laid down all the problems and now you have to navigate your characters through all the twist and turns of the plot to reach the conclusion. Unfortunately, at this point you've forgotten what you've written before and where you were going with the story. What you have to do is keep going and get through to the end. Then go back and edit it later.

Please, Miss, I'm stuck

I speak to many first time writers at conferences and workshops who tell me that were going great guns for a few months but then find themselves stuck. They think it's because they haven't got what it takes to be a novelist but that is just not true. We all get stuck at some point in the story. What you have to do is just keep writing and push through to the end. Then go back and edit it later.

Tell me what you think

Get yourself a good critique partner, not your mum or sister, but someone who knows about the craft of putting together a story and listen to their advice. If they don't get what you are trying to say then neither will an agent nor editor. Believe me, you'll have to learn to take constructive criticism, it comes with the job.

Apprenticeship

It took me three years to develop the skill to become a nurse, and then another four years to become a nurse specialist, so why would it take me any less time to learn how to write a story properly?

There is never enough time

If you wait until you have enough time, the children are grown or when you've retired you'll never write. You have to carve out the time and do it now!

Dyslexia

If you suffer from a degree of dyslexia, as I do, that doesn't stop you becoming a published writer, in fact I would argue it gives you an added bit to your imagination. However, in publishing there are no exception stickers and the spelling and grammar has to be correct in anything you submit. I had to have my manuscripts professionally copy edited before I submitted them and you may have to consider doing the same to get yourself off that slush pile and onto an editor's desk.

Jean Fullerton, author of *No Cure for Love*
(Winner of the 2006 Harry Bowling Prize); *A Glimpse at Happiness.*

19

Revealing All!

Should you show your novel to people you know?

Here's a typical comment from a student. *'I've shown the novel to my husband and he thinks it's wonderful!'*

Similarly, they've said this to me too. *'I've shown the novel to my husband and he thinks the heroine is rather weak.'*

The first comment can fill the writer with misplaced confidence. And the second with misplaced lack of confidence.

I'm afraid my view is that you should never show your novel to friends or family unless they are writers or agents or publishers who might be able to offer some professional, unbiased advice or comment. There is an exception which I will outline in the next section.

And I have to say here that some partners – husbands, wives, partners, children – do feel threatened by their nearest and dearest writing a novel. They might be worried that they could be the subject matter or they might be worried that they are going to 'lose' that person if they become successful.

Now this doesn't, by any means, happen all the time but it is worth bearing in mind. Many writers never show their manuscripts to their loved ones until it's out on the bookshelf. I'm one of these. I just prefer it that way even though, luckily, I have a husband who isn't threatened by my writing. On the other hand, I have a novelist friend who shows her finished manuscript to her husband just in case she has inadvertently based it on someone she knows. He will then say 'I think you'd better change such and such or she might think it is her.'

WRITERS' COURSES AND GROUPS – GOOD IDEA?

Should you join a writers' group? Or go on a course? This is an impossible one to answer because it totally depends on the group. However, I would urge you to consider the following:

- **Writers' groups and writers' courses are two completely different things**. The first is generally a group of people who want to write. They like the idea of getting feedback, which is fine – but remember that just as showing it to friends and family can make you over-confident or lose your confidence, so can writers' groups have the same effect. If they are not professional writers, their advice might not be spot on.

- **Writers' courses vary tremendously in terms of standards**. If you can, find a writers' course that's attached to a university. Some run leisure courses such as the one I teach on at Oxford University. Many run creative writing diplomas in the evening – for details, Google 'creative writing diploma' and check out the area as these are changing all the time. Some local authority classes employ a creative writing teacher too.

- **My advice is to find a teacher who has already been published – preferably in a field that you are interested in**. A teacher who has had an academic book published might not be the best person to help you write a novel. Indeed, I have several students who have had non-fiction published or who have written intellectual papers and reports as part of their work.

But they find it difficult to get out of that mode and become more creative. This is the role of a teacher to help their students get out of what I call 'office speak' through being aware of characterisation, dialogue, plot and all the others things discussed in this book.

LITERARY CONSULTANCIES

There are several literary consultancies around who will – for a fee – look through your novel and write you a written report on what needs to be done before you send it to an agent. Some of these consultancies have links with agents.

The cost can vary from around £30–£50 for the first three chapters, to £300–£500 plus for a 100,000 word plus novel.

Is it worth it? Again, I'm afraid it's difficult to say because it depends on the consultant looking at your novel. But my advice is to find a reputable consultant who has worked full time in the publishing world and/or is a published novelist him/herself.

Also ask them to put you in touch with other students they have helped as a 'reference'. Don't be afraid to do this. After all, you're the customer.

LITERARY FESTIVALS

I wish I'd known about these when I was trying to get published. One of the best literary festivals is Winchester, which is held in the summer for a week. There, writers, publishers and authors gather to give workshops and one-to-one help for anyone trying to get published. I know of people who have been given contracts as a result. For more details, see www.winchesterfestival.co.uk.

WRITERS' HOLIDAYS

These can be useful, fun and lead to contacts. There are several around but I've had experience of the following and think they are definitely worthwhile.

Writers Holidays. www.writersholiday.net
Anne and Gerry Hobbs,
School Bungalow
Church Road,
Pontnewydd,
CWMBRAN,
Torfaen NP44 1AT.
Tel: 01633 489438
E: gerry@writersholiday.net

Skyros Holidays. www.skyros.com

Arvon Foundation. www.arvonfoundation.org

❛ *I read hundreds of submissions every year and I am constantly surprised at how many writers submit work without checking our guidelines first. Whether you are submitting to an agent or a publisher, do your research. Are they interested in the genre of novel you have written? Do they accept unsolicited manuscripts? How do they like work to be submitted? You can find all this information from reference books such as* Writers' and Artists' Yearbook. *Don't inform a publisher that you prefer to send your work in a different format to the one they have requested (yes, it does happen and no, these writers haven't done themselves any favours!).* ❜

Ian Skillicorn, Producer, Short Story Radio. www.ianskillicorn.co.uk

20

How to Get Published

This is the section everyone wants to turn to first! And my first piece of advice is to go back to the beginning of the book where I've talked about how to find your voice and write about something which stands out.

If you can do that, you have a better chance of being different from all the other manuscripts which end up in the daily post to an agent.

But which agent should you send to? the *Writers' and Artists' Year Book* and *The Writers' Handbook* has a list of agents. Go through them and select about half a dozen who deal with the kind of books you write. They usually list which genres they do and don't do; for instance, some won't touch sci-fi.

Then send your first three chapters and a synopsis to each of the agents. Ideally, you are meant to send this to one agent at a time but I've had students who have done this and still been waiting six months later to hear from the first.

Make a note of what you've sent and to whom.

Either send return postage or make it clear that you don't need it back again.

Ensure your manuscript is double spaced and in a readable font: I usually go for Aerial in 12 point. Number the pages and put your name and contact number on the first page.

If you're using a pseudonym, you don't need to say this is a pseudonym at this stage if you don't want to. (By the way, you can pick any name you like but do check (usually through the internet and also the Society of Authors) that there aren't any other authors by that name.)

Keep the covering letter short. Explain what kind of book this is (romantic comedy; thriller, etc) and say what makes it different. If your life experience is relevant, say so, briefly. For instance, if you are writing a comedy about a hospital and you are a nurse, this might be important. Also mention if you have won any writing competitions or if you have been published in other areas.

It can help to include quotes from well-known writers. I know of people who have managed to get published because they've managed to get positive quotes from other writers (whom they know already or have just written to, out of the blue).

IF AT FIRST. . .

Don't be dejected if an agent won't take you on. Simply carry on working through the list in the *Writers' and Artists' Year Book*. It can be very hard to find an agent who is willing to invest his or her time/energy in you, especially in today's climate.

TIP

Try to find an agent who has just set up on his or her own or perhaps recently joined an agency and is keen to make his/her own mark. Groups like the RNA (see below) can tell you about news in the publishing world as can magazines like *Writers' News* and *Writers' Forum*.

❝ *What do agents look for? The following advice might help. Don't be too autobiographical with your first novel. Do think a lot about the plot. It's clear from some submissions that people don't know where the plot is going and that there's a lack of planning. Plotting out a novel before you begin, can work. Although it's not everyone's method, it can help to ensure the plot isn't shambolic and has some structure and order. Sometimes a strong voice will compensate for a rambling plot but not always.*

Pay attention to viewpoint too. Decide who your main character is and stick to it. You can't suddenly change to a different character in the next paragraph. ❞

John Saddler, literary agent.

❝ *I began writing novels partly because my ex married a much younger (and brighter) woman who was doing a BA at Uni because she was determined to write a novel. My daughter bet me I could get a novel published first – so I did! She has yet to be published! I was lucky, I joined the RNA [Romantic Novelists Association] at the instigation of a friend at a writers' group and got a publisher the very first book that went into the New Writers scheme, so I guess I would have to say join the RNA. I read for the scheme now to re-pay their help.* ❞

Anne Styles, author of *The Sins of Sarah*; *That Cinderella Feeling* (both published by Robinson Scarlet). www.annamelindathedizzywife.blogspot.com

❝ *Ignore the niggly voice of doubt in your head. You can do it, you just have to keep going.* ❞

Alex Brown, author.

DO YOU NEED AN AGENT?

Most publishers will only look at a novel if it comes through an agent. However, there are some publishers who will take unsolicited manuscripts. Again, the best advice is to look through the *Writers' and Artists' Yearbook* where publishers will tell you if they take unsolicited manuscripts.

ROMANTIC NOVELISTS ASSOCIATION

I've already mentioned this organisation as a good networking source but they also run the New Writers Scheme. For a fee (£90 at the moment), new members can send their manuscript to someone at the RNA who will read it and provide feedback. If they like it a lot, it will have a second reading and possibly be recommended to an agent.

THE INTERNET

Certain sites like www.youwriteon.com can help writers to be published according to stories I have heard. The idea is that writers post their work on the site and other people vote on whether they like them or not. There are also competitions. Some publishers will look at this work as a showcase so there is a possibility that someone might get picked up.

Other sites include:

Online-novels.blogspot.com. You can put your novel online.

COMPETITIONS

I always advise my students to enter novel competitions – but only if they don't hope they will win. Then, if they do, it's a bonus. Competitions can be a great way of helping someone to write because they provide a discipline (the subject is already given) and a word length which you have to stick to.

writing-about-writing.blogspot.com

Goss First Novel competition: details from www.booksfromscotland.com

Minotaur Books (part of Macmillan) which runs crime competitions. http://us.macmillan.com/ Content.aspx?publisher = minotaurbooks&id = 4933

The Harry Bowling Award. www.harrybowlingprize.net. A wonderful award, established by the family of novelist Harry Bowling, for unpublished novelists. I myself was runner up during the nineties.

DEALING WITH REJECTION

No one likes being rejected. But remember all those well-known novelists who had their manuscripts rejected time and time again before being taken on. Someone once said to me that one difference between a published novelist and an unpublished novelist is that the first one didn't give up.

Having said that, you can learn a lot from feedback from agents and publishers, if they have time to give you that. If you get a nice rejection letter, it's worth contacting them to see if they can tell you how you might improve.

Many writers – myself included – felt they taught themselves through a series of unpublished novels. It's like putting yourself through an apprenticeship because you get stronger, hopefully, as a writer.

Always finish a book. Prove to yourself you can do it. A lot of people stop halfway through. Follow the guidelines that agents give you about presentation. They're all listed in the Writers' *and* Artists' Yearbook.

Identify what kind of book you're writing and try to find an agent who deals with that. Keep your covering letter to the agent short and sweet. Include anything in your life which might help. If you've written a medical novel and you're a surgeon, say so. Present a three line pitch to say what your story is about. Don't go on for four pages. Personal recommendations can help.

Don't email your first three chapters and synopsis. People can forget emails. Post instead.

Talk to writers who have made it. They might have tips. Their experience could gee you up.

First person stories tend to be harder to sell than third person. Don't send it off until you are certain it is well written.

Phil Patterson, agent at Marjacq Scripts.

SELF-PUBLISHING

Self-publishing can be seen as a last resort if you haven't managed to persuade a publisher to publish you. But in fact, publishers have been known to have been so impressed by a self-published novelist that they have then offered the writer a contract. This happened to Jennifer Worth who wrote *Call the Midwife*.

How to self-publish and how much will it cost.
I can't advise you to go to specific people but the following seem to be used regularly by writers for self-publishing.

Author House. www.authorhouse.co.uk

The Book Guild 01273 720900. info@bookguild.co.uk. www.bookguild.co.uk

Lulu. www.lulu.com

www.selfpublishing.com. Includes editorial advice, etc.

www.sparkwave.co.uk. Also includes editorial advice.

> *When you've finished your first novel and polished it as much as you can, set it aside and write another. Do not submit the first one to a publisher yet.*
>
> *Once you've written the second novel, go back to No 1 and you'll see how to improve it hugely. Only then should you submit it.*

Anna Jacobs, author of *Freedom's Land, Farewell to Lancashire, Chestnut Lane, Saving Willowbrook* and *In Focus*.

TIP

Accept that your first novel may not be successful and grow a thick enough skin for it not to matter. Start another while you wait for a response from a publisher, so you have a 'new baby' for consolation if the first does not succeed. Write something every day and read the previous day's work before starting again. I often stop in the middle of a sentence (or paragraph) to make starting again more fluent. When I have finished something, I put it away for a few days and do something quite different. This way I can actually see some of the errors and typos with a fresh eye.

❛ *In order to get published, bear the following points in mind:*

Put your characters on the stage and write what you see. You're in the front row of that audience. Picture them in front of you from the way they move to the way they talk.

Don't just write dialogue like a script. Include narrative. Have a healthy mix of both!

When it comes to viewpoint, I think third person works best. However, the first person can also work, depending on your voice and the kind of novel you are writing. You need to try them out.

If you want to write a saga, look at other sagas in bookshops. Think of an area which hasn't been done before but don't pick one that's too obscure.

Don't have too much internal dialogue. And don't make your thoughts 'baggy'.

Listen! If you are writing about teenagers or young people, go out and into areas where your age groups go and listen to the things they say and the way they say them.

Write about what you know.

One of the biggest mistakes from inexperienced writers, is to over-write. Take out anything that's not necessary for the story.'

Betty Schwartz, freelance editor (formerly Hodder & Stoughton).

❛*Some people say that it's a good idea to find a small publisher because they pay you more attention. But first you have to find your agent. When you've squirrelled through the* Writers' and Artists' Yearbook, *ring the agent first before you send your ms (manuscript) to check they are still taking on submissions. Otherwise it could be a waste of your postage.*'

Sara Banerji, writing tutor and author of *Shining Hero* (Harper Collins) and *The Waiting Time* (Transita).

❛1. Write the book you want to read. *This sounds obvious, but you'd be surprised how many authors think they can just 'bash out' a novel. But the fact is you absolutely have to write a book that you'd actually enjoy yourself, or your book will have no depth, truth or marketability about it. Which, as every reader knows, actually matters. Imagine Jodi Picoult without the tough moral choices and powerful characterisation, Jeffery Deaver without the pace and drama, Marian Keyes without the warmth? They just wouldn't be the same.*

2. Be determined but realistic. *Believing in yourself is vital to getting yourself noticed. But don't ignore criticism. Many authors*

write several drafts (or indeed totally different novels) before they write the one that gets them that coveted publishing deal.

3. Ask your first readers to be honest. *Before you send the manuscript out, do get your friends to read it – but only if you 100% trust them to tell you what they really think. If they're too nice (!), maybe think about joining a writers' group for some constructive criticism. Because often outsiders can spot things you didn't notice were a problem – such as holes in the plot, or places where characterisation needs to be beefed up.*

4. Find the perfect agent for you and your book. *Agents can really help: editorially, supportively and, most importantly, to help you find that deal. Plus there are some brilliant ones out there. Why not look in the acknowledgements of your favourite authors' novels and see who their agent is? Or try the* Writers' and Artists' Yearbook *for a comprehensive list of literary agencies.*

5. Be a professional from the outset. *This sounds like a really minor point, but it really makes a difference. So, at the start, if a publisher says they don't accept unsolicited manuscripts, or an agent says they only want the first three chapters (in Times New Roman, font size 12, double spaced with large margins, etc.!) do take their advice. A crazy font doesn't make your book more likely to be noticed. What does is a strong covering letter and a really good book. And if you're professional, they are more likely to respond in kind.*

6. Do not lose heart. *The path to being published might feel impossible but real talent does have a way of making it along that path, so please – new writers – don't give up!*

Isobel Akenhead, editor at Hodder & Stoughton.

21

Writing the Next Novel

This might feel like the last thing you want to do – and if it is, it might be that you're not a writer. Most writers have all kinds of ideas for the next novel running through their head. And this is a good thing! If a publisher is interested in you, they might well call you and your agent into an editorial meeting and one of the things he or she will want to know, is what other ideas you have.

One piece of advice I was given by an agent after my first novel, was to write the next one 'while you are waiting for the first one to be accepted'. In fact, the first one wasn't accepted (although it got lots of nice encouraging rejection letters) but it was a good bit of advice to write another. It helps to take your mind off the first doing its rounds. And, as I've said, you will hopefully be a better writer because you will be more aware of viewpoint, characterisation and plot, etc.

'*Apply yourself. It took me 15 years to get my first book published because I kept stopping and starting, re-writing the beginning and not finishing it, and going off and doing other things for months on end. Be determined and persistent to push on to the end of the book. Then you have a piece of work that you can start to edit.* '

Nicola Cornick, author of several novels, including *The Undoing of A Lady* from HQN Books.

' *The first 2000 words is easy – it's the last 98,000 that can be tough... Application is everything. Bottom on seat! Join the RNA to get an outside pair of eyes. Don't give it to your family to read. You need someone you can trust to comment on it. Someone who will be brutal. Read your dialogue out loud. If you're going to write in a certain genre like Mills & Boon or Little Black Dress, read everything you can that's been published by them.*'

Kate Lace, author of *The Love Boat*, Little Black Dress.

' *Read a lot. Analyse how plots work and what characters are up to. Review, review, review! I never regard my first draft as anything but preliminary skirmish with the page. I've been surprised by people who reckon a book is finished the day they compete the first draft. I only know what I mean to say when I've read what I've said! My first novel was 500 pages that I dashed off under the desk at work in under a year. Now I can take between two and three years to write a novel. It doesn't matter how long it takes as long as it's the best you can do.*'

Margaret Pelling, author of *Work For Four Hands*, Starborn Books.

22

Don't Skip This! It might help...

DEFINITIONS

Ms: manuscript.

WIP: Work in progress.

Advance: The amount of money you are paid when a book is accepted. This can be anything from £1000 – over £50,000.

Royalties: this is what you earn once you have 'earned out' your advance. In other words, sold so many books that you have earned the equivalent of your advance (remember that many bookshops sell novels at discount rates so this can take a while).

Genre: what kind of novel is it, e.g. thriller; historical.

Protagonist: main character.

Show and not tell: make the reader feel they are there with the characters, rather than just telling the story from a distance. See Chapter 11.

Conflict and resolution: this is just a fancy way of saying that you need a problem for your novel – or else there is no story! Hopefully, by now, you'll know that. But if not, here's a checklist:

Without a problem, there is no story!

A character needs a problem to develop.

A story needs a problem to keep going.

One problem isn't enough.

In a novel, you have space and time to resolve a problem. But a short story needs to be able to be solved in a page or two at the most.

A problem can't be too serious in a short story. But it needs to be believable and have punch.

The solution needs to be believable. Don't give yourself such a bad problem that you can't solve it.

COMMONLY ASKED QUESTIONS

How long does it take to write a novel?
It takes me about four to six months to write a first draft and then two or three more months to do a second and maybe a third. Some people take much longer and others shorter. But it's important to write regularly to keep up the flow.

Should I talk about my novel to people?
If you do, there's a danger that someone might take the idea. I don't think it's sensible as it takes away the need to tell the story on keyboard or on paper if you tell someone what it's about.

How much will I be paid for a first novel?
Usually between £1000 and £50,000 although it could be more. Publishers normally offer a two-book deal, which means the money is for two novels; you are then committed to writing the

second. However, the publisher isn't committed to publishing it if it's not acceptable.

What is an advance?

An advance is the name given to the initial payment by the publisher – such as the figure given above.

When do I get royalties?

Not until you have 'earned out' your advance. This can take time because books are often sold so cheaply now. So don't presume that if you have an advance of £5000 and your novels sell for £5.99, you just divide the first figure by the second!

Do I need to pay an agent?

No. An agent will take a percentage of the money received from a publisher – if it is accepted. This percentage is generally 10 per cent. That's why it's so difficult to be accepted by an agent. He or she needs to be convinced about selling you otherwise it's a waste of time.

Do I have to see a lawyer before getting a pen name?

No. You can pick any name, although it's advisable not to have one that's already in use. You don't need to tell anyone about the pen name until your novel is accepted.

How can I publicise my novel – especially if it's self-published?

Some self-publishers offer a service whereby they help you publicise your novel. But even if you're published by a mainstream publisher, it can help if you do something to spread the word. Make sure copies are sent well in advance to magazines and newspapers so they get there in time for deadlines. Think of articles you could write about your novel and suggest them as magazine and newspaper ideas. Offer to give talks to societies. For more advice, read *Marketing Your Book; an Author's Guide* by Alison Baverstock.

What is a mainstream publisher?
It's a publisher who is well known in the book world such as Orion or Hodder or Random House.

What is an imprint?
It's a section within that house. For example, Black Swan is part of Transworld.

I've started writing a novel but I've just seen that someone else has had a novel published, using a similar idea. Does that mean I've wasted my time?
Not necessarily. Although it would help if yours had a different angle. Remember that if your novel is accepted, it will take about one to two years before it is published. So an agent and publisher might feel that if your novel is really good, it will still stand out.

USEFUL ORGANISATIONS
Public Lending Rights
This is an organisation which will collect money due to you, if your books are borrowed from the library. So if you do have a book published (it can be fiction or non-fiction), it's essential to register. You can do this, by going onto www.plr.uk.com

The Society of Authors
This is open to anyone who has had a book published. It runs excellent talks, meetings and a very good contract service whereby experts examine your contract with a publisher to check it is fair. www.societyof authors.org

The Authors' Licensing and Collecting Society
Another organisation which helps you collect money owed to you
as an author, often through photocopies. www.alcs.co.uk.
Tel: 0207 264 5700.

The Romantic Novelists Association
This is an excellent organisation which runs regular national and
regional events. It is open to both unpublished and published
writers and offers a New Writers Scheme, under which you can
send in a novel or part of a novel, for advice (price included in the
annual fee). www.rna-uk.org

The Crime Writers Association
Open to published writers of crime although it also runs
competitions for writers of unpublished novels.
www.the cwa.co.uk

www.bbc.co.uk/writersroom/ Fantastic site which is bursting with
ideas for writers.

www.write-invite.com Writers' group, running competitions, talks
and giving advice.

www.unpublishedauthorsbookshop.co.uk. A website which helps
unpublished authors.

Index

advance, 197
agent, 11, 16, 49, 136, 166, 171,
    179, 183–5, 186, 192, 197
agony aunt pages, 32
alliteration, 175

beginning, 46–53, 78, 98
blurb, 171

Call the Midwife, 189
characters, 70, 83–99, 174
    animals, 92–3
    baddy, 93
    believable, 89–90
    minor, 94
    names, 94–5
    relatives, 92
    seasonal dates, 96
'coat hanger techniques', 61
colour, 148
competitions, 187
computer, 168
    back-up, 10, 168
covering letter, 184, 192
creative writing diploma, 180

Desperate Housewives, 113

dialogue, 11, 190
Dr Wicked's writing lab, 3
dyslexia, 178

edit, 11, 168, 189
editor, 168, 174
ending, 51–2, 78, 79

film, 23
first person, 40, 107–10, 188,
    190
first sentence, 46–53
Five People You Meet in Heaven,
    50
flashbacks, 31, 80–1
flash fiction, 7–9, 39
foreshadowing, 98

genres, 16, 40, 158–60
*Guernsey Literary and Potato
    Peel Pie Society*, 175

Hodder & Stoughton, 12, 167
*How to Write Short Stories and
    Get Published*, 21
humour, 22, 63, 153–7

ideas, 5, 16–36, 166, 170, 198
   identifying, 17, 22, 47
   magazines and newspapers,
      28–33
   old themes, 24–5
   real life, 17–23
   television and radio, 9, 33–4
   wow, 26
Ideas book, 1, 48, 62
internal dialogue, 139, 190
internet, 186

Kennedy, Bernadine, 174
Kinsella, Sophie, 17

learning process, 3
literary consultancies, 181
literary festivals, 181
location, *see* place
loose ends, 66, 75

magazines, 8, 28, 30, 89, 197
manuscript, 172, 183, 192
Marketing Your Book: an
   Author's Guide, 198
music, 10

newspapers, 28, 30, 197

omniscient narrator, 107

pay, 196
pen name, *see* pseudonym

place, 9, 11–12
plot, 54–82
'plot pusher' 8, 20, 23, 71, 93
plotting
   A–Z method, 68–71
   believable, 56–7, 196
   mechanics, 58
   outline, 171
   revision, 167
   throw and scatter, 71
   tree diagram, 72–7
   twist, 24, 115
   'up the ante', 55–6, 82
   and viewpoint, 114
   whiteboard, 72
Pride and Prejudice, 57, 93
print out, 66, 167
problem, 22, 23, 54–5, 85, 196
pseudonym, 184, 197
publicity, 197

red pen, 66, 167
rejection, 12, 187
research, 25, 80
revision, 66, 166–70
Romantic Novelists Association
   (RNA), 185, 186, 194, 199
royalties, 197

School Run, The, 12, 39, 147,
   155
Second Time Lucky, 52, 171
self-publishing, 189, 197

setting, 26, 131–7
Shell Seekers, The, 152
short stories, 21–2
smells, 9, 131, 147–8
Society of Authors, 184
sounds, 9, 131, 148
strong words, 138, 142
sub-plot, 57
Supper Club, The, 85–6, 89, 92,
    154, 162
synopsis, 171–4, 183

taste, 149
Taylor Bradford, Barbara, 29
tension, 26, 56, 59
third person, 40, 107, 110–12,
    188
time, 3, 4, 13–14
timeline, 161–5
    seasons, 163
    special occasions, 162
    years, 164
Time Traveller's Wife, The, 37

title, 175–8
touch, 149

viewpoint, 101–17, 185, 190, 193
voice, 37–45, 60, 174, 185

Wedding Party, The, 39, 41, 47,
    54, 59–61, 65, 73, 94, 103,
    134, 172
Weldon, Fay, 37
Woman of Substance, A, 29
Writers' and Artists' Yearbook,
    182, 183, 184, 188, 191, 192
writers' block, 7–10, 66
writers' courses, 180
writers' groups, 7, 180, 192
Writers' Handbook, The, 183
Writers' Holiday, 5, 182
Writers' Forum, 184
Writers' News, 184
writing buddies, 41
writing tools, 10–11

WRITING FOR CHILDREN
PAMELA CLEAVER

This new edition combines Pamela Cleaver's bestselling *Writing a Children's Book* with her *Ideas for Children's Writers*. In it you will learn about plotting and planning, beginnings, middles and endings, how to research and how to revise and how to find a publisher. There is no one right way to write a children's book but if you are armed with a knowledge of certain techniques that have worked for other writers you will be more likely to succeed.

ISBN 978-1-84528-330-8

HOW TO WRITE SHORT STORIES FOR MAGAZINES
SOPHIE KING

'An invaluable source of tips and inside information from writers and magazines editors.' – *Good Book Guide*

This book will take you as a would-be writer through the tricks of the trade by helping you discover what the different magazines are looking for and how to think up ideas to suit; demonstrating how you can write different slants, such as twist in the tales and feel-good stories; advising on how you can win fiction competitions.

ISBN 978-1-84528-385-8

CREATIVE WRITING

How to unlock your imagination, develop your writing skills – and get published
ADÈLE RAMET

'This is a book which merits a place on every writer's bookshelf.'
– *Writers' Bulletin*

'...an excellent book for the beginner writer. Packed with examples and case studies, this is not a book that just deals in theory.' – *Writers' News*

This book is a first-rate guide for writers who are looking for ways to improve their output.

ISBN 978-1-84528-402-2

WRITING FROM LIFE

LYNNE HACKLES

'I suggest you take it with you when you travel to work . . . You will begin thinking and often those are the moments to begin a new journey. The book will prod you onward. Highly recommended.'
– *www.london-morning-paper.co.uk*

'Her excellent book demonstrates that writing about what you know really is the way into print, whether you are writing non-fiction or fiction.' – *Writing Magazine*

'Practical techniques that will make it easier.' – *Good Book Guide*

ISBN 978-1-84528-419-0

THE CREATIVE WRITER'S WORKBOOK
CATHY BIRCH

'...exudes confidence and optimism...full of devices to make the imagination flow.' – *Alison Chisholm, BBC Radio Merseyside*

'Your true writer's voice is unlikely to inhabit the realms of logic...this book takes you on a journey into the subconscious to help you find that voice – and use it. The results can be both amazing and satisfying.' – *Writer's Own*

'There is a solid, practical base to this book...Give Cathy's methods a try, you might surprise yourself.' – *Writers' Bulletin*

ISBN 978-1-84528-306-3

THE BEGINNER'S GUIDE TO GETTING PUBLISHED
CHRISS MCCALLUM

'Absorbing and highly informative...No author seriously interested in getting published can afford to be without this book.' – *Writers' News*

'Really definitive...Leaves every other similar book in its shade.' – *Pause, National Poetry Foundation*

'Worth every penny. If you're really serious about being published, this book should be your bible.' – *Writers' Bulletin*

'...should be on any beginner's reading list.' – *Writers Forum*

ISBN 978-1-85703-217-2

THE FIVE-MINUTE WRITER
MARGRET GERAGHTY

'I purchased this book on a whim, hoping to obtain some creative genius to help me write. I was pleasantly surprised by how much it helped me in my time of great need to achieve ideas and comfort me in my period of writers block.
Outstanding work by Geraghty... I attribute (hopefully) my success in the future.
A must for first-time writers! ' – *Reader review*

'An exploration of ritualistic behaviour, thinking outside the box, writing about the concept of choice. Just three of the 57 topics and they are presented in a way that stimulates your creative thinking process.'
– *Writing Magazine*

This book will inspire you to write – even if you have only a few minutes a day to spare. Each chapter offers you a writing-related discussion, followed by a five-minute exercise. Just pick a page and begin your writer's journey.

ISBN 978-1-84528-339-1

HOW TO WRITE A THRILLER

SCOTT MARIANI

'I just wish this book had been around when I was starting out. It's highly engaging, inspirational and full of useful insights... just like a great thriller itself, I couldn't put it down! Reading this book should be the first step for any budding thriller writer', 'highly engaging, inspirational and full of useful insights...' – *Seth Garner*, author of *The Blood Partnership* and *Broken Surface*

ISBN 978-1-84528-163-2

How To Books are available through all good bookshops, or you can order direct from us through Grantham Book Services.

Tel: +44 (0)1476 541080
Fax: +44 (0)1476 541061
Email: orders@gbs.tbs-ltd.co.uk

Or via our website

www.howtobooks.co.uk

To order via any of these methods please quote the title(s) of the book(s) and your credit card number together with its expiry date.

For further information about our books and catalogue, please contact:

How To Books
Spring Hill House,
Spring Hill Road,
Begbroke
Oxford OX5 1RX,

Visit our web site at

www.howtobooks.co.uk

Or you can contact us by email at info@howtobooks.co.uk